Therapy Games for Kids

Therapy GAMES FOR KIDS

100 Activities to Boost Self-Esteem, Improve Communication, and Build Coping Skills

Christine Kalil, LICSW, RPT

No book, including this one, can ever replace the diagnostic expertise and medical advice of a physician in providing information about your health. The information contained herein is not intended to replace medical advice. You should consult with your doctor before using the information in this or any health-related book.

First Rockridge Press trade paperback edition 2022

For general information on our other products and services, please contact our Customer Care Department within the United States at (866) 744-2665, or outside the United States at (510) 253-0500.

Paperback ISBN: 978-1-63878-731-0 | eBook ISBN: 978-1-68539-114-0

Manufactured in the United States of America

Interior and Cover Designer: Gabe Nansen
Art Producer: Janice Ackerman
Editor: Andrea Leptinsky
Production Editor: Matthew Burnett
Production Manager: Riley Hoffman

0 1 2 3 4 5 6 7 8 9 10

This book is dedicated to my mother, from whom I learned my love of service; my father, who has supported me throughout my career even when I was unsure; and my clients, whose spirits and resilience inspire me to do this work.

Contents

Introduction

Because children's brains are still growing, they learn best through games and play rather than through talking. As Fred Rogers said, "Play is often talked about as if it were a relief from serious learning. But for children, play is serious learning." This fact led to the creation of play therapy as a tool to help children deal with emotional issues and to learn new coping skills. Rather than talking about how to handle a problem, play allows them to practice it, which leads to better learning.

This book will focus on prescriptive play therapy tools, which means that the games are created with a specific lesson or goal in mind. The activities pull primarily from cognitive behavioral therapy (CBT), which research consistently shows to be effective for treating issues such as anxiety, depression, and many others.

As a child therapist for the past 15 years, play therapy has been my most powerful tool. I have seen it help children grow and heal, become kinder and more patient, improve their ability to problem-solve and express themselves, and feel more confident that they can handle challenges in life. It benefits all children: those in foster care, hospitals, schools, and private practices. The games in this book are powerful because children learn best when they are having fun and when you give them your full attention.

I am incredibly excited to share some of my tools with you so that you can also see the magic that happens when children have an open, supportive, and fun space in which to connect with themselves. You will find that the activities in this book use mostly inexpensive and easy-to-find materials so that you can use the activities easily at home, in a school, or in an office.

How to Use This Book

This book is for therapists, counselors, and caregivers of children ages 8 to 12. The games in this book will help children build skills so that they can deal with common challenges such as anxiety, bullying, grief, and more. For accessibility purposes, the activities use basic and inexpensive materials. However, the games vary slightly in difficulty, so each game lists a difficulty level from 1 to 3. For ease of use, each chapter focuses on a particular challenge, and the activities increase in difficulty within the chapter. Lastly, at the end of each game, you'll find helpful tips and discussion questions. Of course, feel free to adjust the games and discussions to suit your needs.

I believe this is a great opportunity for adults to model healthy communication, expression of feelings, and more to guide our young participants. That said, since we need to model the traits that we want to teach, it's important to do your own self-care. When you're fully present, the activities in this book are an amazing opportunity for learning and connection.

Finally, these games are not meant to be used in place of therapy. If you are concerned about a child's mental health, please seek help from a mental health professional. I hope that you enjoy using these games as much as I have, but most importantly, have fun!

CHAPTER ONE

Making Mindful Choices

Mindfulness means present-moment awareness. It is normal to feel stressed sometimes, but too much stress means children aren't learning, and are instead in a state of tension and worry. Practicing mindfulness encourages a state of moment-to-moment awareness where children can access a state of calm, in which learning and growth can take place. Mindfulness can seem hard at first, but like anything else, a child can get better at it with practice. These activities can help!

TO THE CLOUDS

ABOUT THE GAME

This game will encourage kids to use their senses to stay in the present moment. They can also use their imagination to help their brains feel calm. In this activity, use colored shaving cream to "paint" an imaginary happy place.

Game Materials
White trash bags, scissors, tape, bowls, shaving cream, food coloring, paintbrushes

Time Needed
20 minutes

Who's Playing?
Any number

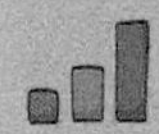

Difficulty
Level 1

Helpful Tips

Use fingerpaint instead of dye to avoid a mess.

Encourage using hands! Get messy!

HOW TO PLAY

1. For each player, cut a trash bag open along one long side and the bottom so that it lays flat when opened. Tape the corners of the trash bag to the workspace.
2. Fill bowls with 2 cups of shaving cream, and mix in 5 drops of food coloring. Mix a bowl for each color.
3. Use the trash bag as a canvas. Using hands or paintbrushes, instruct players to "paint" a scene (real or pretend) that would be happiest to them.
4. When finished, have the child describe their scene to you or other players. Describe:
   - 5 things to see
   - 4 things to hear
   - 3 things to feel
   - 2 things to smell
   - 1 thing to taste

LET'S TALK ABOUT IT!

When you next have a bad day, how can this activity help cheer you up?

WISHFUL THINKING

ABOUT THE GAME

Some things can't be controlled, but kids can learn to use positive thinking to boost moods and focus energy on good things. In this activity, children will make a time capsule to create wishes for the year.

Game Materials
Jar or bottle, paper, drawing materials, paint

Time Needed
15 to 20 minutes

Who's Playing?
1 or more people

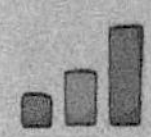

Difficulty
Level 1

Helpful Tip

This activity is great for the start of a new school year or at the beginning of the calendar year.

HOW TO PLAY

1. Write or draw the following wishes for the next year: a wish for the child, their family, their neighborhood, their country, and the world.
2. Have players write down or draw something that they're looking forward to this year.
3. Just for fun, write down a prediction.
4. Put the wishes and drawings inside the jar and close the top.
5. Use paint (or any other materials you have, such as ribbons, jewels, or stickers) to decorate the outside of the jar.
6. Write the date on the jar.
7. Save the wishes and see if they come true at the end of the year!

LET'S TALK ABOUT IT!

What can you do to make it more likely that some of your wishes will come true?

IT'S A BIRD! IT'S A PLANE!

ABOUT THE GAME

Worries are a normal part of life, but too much worrying can make bodies feel tired or even sick. In this activity, children will help their bodies relax by breathing and playing with paper airplanes.

Game Materials
Piece of paper, pencil

Time Needed
10 minutes

Who's Playing?
Any number of people

Difficulty
Level 1

Helpful Tip

Try out different styles of airplanes. Find instructions easily by searching the internet.

HOW TO PLAY

1. Have each player take one piece of paper and write or draw something that has been worrying them.
2. Fold the paper into a paper airplane.
3. Once they have made their airplane, take it to a place where it can fly. This is best done outside, if possible.
4. Taking turns, have each player fly their airplane in the following way:
    - Take a deep breath in through their nose.
    - Count to four in their head and imagine their worries leaving their body.
    - Throw their airplane.
    - Breathe out through their mouth as slowly as possible.
5. Repeat for as long as the players like and make as many planes as time allows.

LET'S TALK ABOUT IT!

What is something that you'd like to let go of that you're comfortable sharing? How would that help you?

VACATION SENSATIONS

ABOUT THE GAME

The brain is very powerful. It can relax just by thinking of something relaxing. Have kids use this guessing game to explore how their five main senses contribute to relaxation.

Game Materials
Piece of paper, pencil

Time Needed
10 minutes

Who's Playing?
2 or more people

Difficulty
Level 2

Helpful Tip

If players can't remember the five senses, write them down where everyone can see.

HOW TO PLAY

1. The first player will think of a place that makes them happy. The place should be known to other players. For example, a player could choose the beach or the park, but not a specific beach or park. (Youngest player goes first.)
2. Player 2 will ask questions about the five main senses. For example:
   - What do they see?
   - What do they smell?
   - What do they taste?
   - What do they hear?
   - What do they feel?
3. If a player thinks they have the answer, a guess counts in the place of a question.
4. See if players can guess the place in 20 questions or less.

LET'S TALK ABOUT IT!

Why do you enjoy the place you chose? How does it feel to imagine being there?

BUT AT LEAST . . .

ABOUT THE GAME

It's important for kids to know that it is okay to be sad when things don't go their way and not to get stuck in negative thinking. Use this game to practice finding something positive in a tough situation.

Game Materials
Balloon,
permanent marker

Time Needed
15 minutes

Who's Playing?
2 or more people

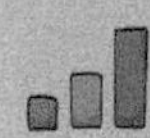

Difficulty
Level 2

Helpful Tip

Use silly situations like "My dog got lost on his way to Mars, but at least . . . "

HOW TO PLAY

1. Blow up the balloon, draw three sections using the marker, and write one of these phrases in each section:
    - But at least ____.
    - But this might help me learn ____.
    - And I have ____ to help me.
2. Have players stand in a circle and give one player the balloon.
3. Instruct the player with the balloon to briefly describe a situation that would cause a negative feeling (annoyed, angry, etc.) and then throw the balloon to the player to their right.
4. When the player catches the balloon, have the player read the phrase in the section that is touching their right thumb and fill in the blank to finish the sentence.
5. Repeat.

LET'S TALK ABOUT IT!

When would it be helpful to have a more open mind?

CALM DOWN UPSIDE DOWN

ABOUT THE GAME

Spending some time upside down can help to calm. Through this activity, kids can experiment with being "heels over head" in a safe manner, see how it feels, and experience the calming effects that it offers.

Game Materials
Timer

Time Needed
10 minutes

Who's Playing?
2 people

Difficulty
Level 2

Helpful Tip

If there are concerns about getting the wall dirty, have participants place their feet over a yoga ball or chair instead.

HOW TO PLAY

1. Have everyone find their pulse on their wrist or neck and take their pulse for 1 minute. Have each player write down their number.
2. Instruct participants to take off their shoes, find a wall, and lay with their back on the floor and their legs extended straight up the wall. Each player's bottom should be at the corner of the floor and the wall.
3. Practice deep breathing for 3 minutes. Instruct each participant to breathe in through their nose for four seconds, hold their breath for two seconds, and breathe out through their mouth as slowly as possible.
4. Have participants remain in the same position, take their pulse again for 1 minute, and note the difference between the two pulse numbers.

LET'S TALK ABOUT IT!

Did your pulse change? Did being "heels over head" feel relaxing?

IT'S NEVER FOREVER

ABOUT THE GAME

Sometimes when someone experiences a bad feeling, it can feel like that feeling will never go away. This activity helps participants practice being in the moment and remember that most things will pass.

Game Materials
Rice, 4 plastic bags, measuring cups and spoons, vinegar, baking sheet, paper towels, paper

Time Needed
20 minutes

Who's Playing?
1 or more people

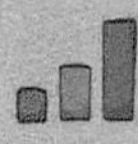

Difficulty
Level 2

Helpful Tip

Use colored sand to save time or color the rice ahead of time.

HOW TO PLAY

1. In each bag, put 1 cup of rice, 1 teaspoon of vinegar, and 4 drops of food coloring.
2. Close the bag and mix.
3. Cover the baking sheet with paper towels and pour each bag of rice into a pile. Spread rice into a thin layer. (This may temporarily stain participant's hands.)
4. Have participants use the rice to create a pattern or figure on a sheet of paper. Encourage them to explore their five senses while doing so: smell the vinegar, feel the texture of the rice, and so on.
5. Ask each child to share their experience with the group. Then, pour the colored rice into a bag to save, or throw it away.

LET'S TALK ABOUT IT!

Feelings, like the drawings, don't last forever. Have you ever had a feeling that seemed like it would last forever?

OFF TO THE RACES!

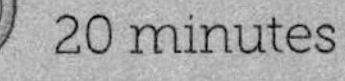

ABOUT THE GAME

The key to using breathing to calm the body is to make the exhale as long as possible. In this activity, participants will practice exhaling while trying to get their cotton ball "horse" farther down the track.

Game Materials
Trash bag, play dough, cotton balls, permanent marker

Time Needed
20 minutes

Who's Playing?
2 or more people

Difficulty
Level 3

Helpful Tip

If you have more than two players, try having a commentator and name the horses.

HOW TO PLAY

1. Lay the trash bag flat on a table.
2. Roll play dough into long, worm-like strands ½ inch thick.
3. Use the dough to make a windy "racetrack" by placing the strands end to end with another piece parallel.
4. Have participants take turns to see how far they can blow their cotton ball down the track with just one breath.
5. Mark each player's finishing point by writing their initials on the bag with the marker.
6. Whoever pushes their "horse" farthest down the track wins the race.
7. Decide on how many rounds to play and keep score to see who wins the most races.

LET'S TALK ABOUT IT!

Can you think of any situations where deep breathing could help you?

SHAKE IT OUT

ABOUT THE GAME

Feelings and memories are stored in the body. Movement can help the body let go of bad feelings. Have kids try this challenge to get their bodies moving and see how many movements the group can remember.

Game Materials
None

Time Needed
10 minutes

Who's Playing?
3 or more people

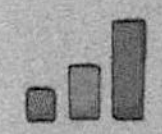

Difficulty
Level 3

Helpful Tips

Encourage silliness.

Give hints if players have a hard time.

HOW TO PLAY

1. Have players stand in a circle.
2. Instruct Player 1 to make any movement they desire to wiggle or stretch their body. The movement can be from as small as a nose wiggle or eyebrow raise to as big as shaking both arms and legs.
3. The player to their left (clockwise) then copies the movement and adds their own.
4. Continue around the circle adding a movement each time.
5. If a player cannot remember the order of the movements, the previous players will do their movements again in order.
6. Proceed until participants complete a circuit.

LET'S TALK ABOUT IT!

Did you notice stress anywhere in your body?

Did you feel different after moving and stretching?

WALK, DON'T TALK

ABOUT THE GAME

This activity will encourage kids to take a walk in nature and focus on the moment. They will then use items that they collected on their walk to make art and challenge others to guess what they made.

Game Materials
Paper, hot glue gun, drawing/painting materials

Time Needed
20 minutes

Who's Playing?
2 or more people

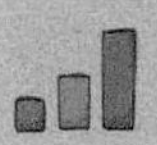

Difficulty
Level 3

Helpful Tips

Play relaxing music while the players create.

Use cardstock instead of paper if possible.

Help with the glue!

HOW TO PLAY

1. Go to a place outside where players can walk and collect small items such as bark, flowers, or rocks.
2. Have players spend five minutes walking quietly and collecting small items from nature.
3. Encourage players to notice the sights, sounds, smells, and textures surrounding them.
4. Instruct players to hot glue collected items onto paper and use art supplies to create a picture of a person who seems calm and confident. It can be a specific person (like a family member or a friend) or a type of person (such as an astronaut or a teacher).
5. Have players take turns sharing and having players guess what each player has created. Give hints until someone guesses correctly.

LET'S TALK ABOUT IT!

How do you feel when you're in nature?

CHAPTER TWO

Building Strong Self-Esteem

Self-esteem means acceptance and love of self. It is possible to improve and grow, but it's okay to be imperfect. Some people may think that self-esteem means a confidence in one's abilities, but it is not necessary to be good at everything to love oneself. The activities in this chapter will help participants practice noticing things they like about themselves, accepting imperfection, and having confidence to try new things.

THAT'S A WRAP!

ABOUT THE GAME

Helping kids identify their strengths is one way to build self-esteem. Here, kids are encouraged to think of proud moments while unwrapping a ball of surprises.

Game Materials
Paper, scissors, plastic wrap, candy, two dice, pen

Time Needed
20 minutes

Who's Playing?
3 to 6 people

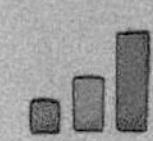

Difficulty
Level 1

Helpful Tip

Make sure everyone gets a turn and bring extra candy.

HOW TO PLAY

1. Cut paper into 20 small squares. Randomly write 1, 2, or 3 (points) on each square.
2. Using the entire roll of plastic wrap, shape the plastic into a ball, placing pieces of candy and torn bits of paper randomly inside the ball.
3. Have the players sit in a circle.
4. Instruct Player 1 to start unwrapping the ball, keeping whatever paper falls out. As they start to earn slips of paper, ask the player to describe a moment of pride to the group.
5. After Player 1 unwraps the ball, instruct the player to their left to roll two dice. When they roll doubles, the dice and the ball are passed again to the left.
6. Continue until the ball is unwrapped.
7. Ask players add up the points from the papers they found in the ball. The player with the most points wins.

LET'S TALK ABOUT IT!

When did you feel proud even if you didn't succeed?

CHANGE IT UP

ABOUT THE GAME

An important part of feeling confident is working through change. Participants will practice staying calm when their drawing is changed and a new plan is needed.

Game Materials
Paper,
drawing materials

Time Needed
15 minutes

Who's Playing?
2 people

Difficulty
Level 1

Helpful Tip

For a challenge, try adding more than one shape or gluing on a googly eye or pom-pom instead.

HOW TO PLAY

1. Give each player a sheet of paper and drawing materials.
2. Instruct players to think of an object to draw and picture the finished drawing in their head.
3. Each player draws the first two lines of their drawing.
4. Ask players to exchange drawings.
5. Each player draws a small circle (about the size of a quarter) on their partner's paper and returns the drawing.
6. Challenge each player to change the plan for their drawing to include the new circle. They can change their first plan or come up with a whole new idea.

LET'S TALK ABOUT IT!

How did you feel when someone changed your plan?

Have you experienced a big change? What did you do?

RED LIGHT, GRATEFUL LIGHT

ABOUT THE GAME

Teaching children to focus on things that make them feel grateful is a great way to help their brains feel peaceful. This activity will challenge kids to name things that make them feel grateful with a twist on "Red Light, Green Light."

Game Materials
None

Time Needed
5 minutes

Who's Playing?
3 to 5 people

Difficulty
Level 1

Helpful Tips

If playing more than one round, the winner becomes the new stoplight.

Play outside if you can.

HOW TO PLAY

1. One player is chosen to be the stoplight. Other players line up across the room.
2. The host will yell, "Grateful light!" The players may begin moving forward, but they must name something for which they're grateful for each step.
3. The stoplight yells, "Yellow light!" or "Red light!" at any point. Players can continue moving forward on yellow light but must do so in slow motion and speak in slow motion. On red light, players freeze.
4. If the host notices that someone is breaking a rule, that player is sent back to the starting line.
5. The first player to reach the stoplight wins.

LET'S TALK ABOUT IT!

Are there any things that you sometimes forget to appreciate?

How can you show appreciation?

COLORFUL YOU

ABOUT THE GAME

This activity will teach children how to use their imagination to change how they are feeling. They will use cotton swabs to paint their feelings and then repeat the exercise while imagining a strong and confident feeling.

Game Materials
Cotton swabs, plates, paint, paper

Time Needed
20 minutes

Who's Playing?
2 to 5 people

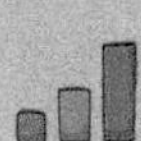

Difficulty
Level 1

Helpful Tip

Cardstock and acrylic paint are great for this activity, but even fingerpaint works.

HOW TO PLAY

1. Instruct each player to fold a piece of paper in half.
2. On the left side, players should use the cotton swabs dipped in paint to cover the page with dots of color to show how they're feeling. On the right side, players should paint what it would look like to feel strong and powerful.
3. Explain that there's no right way to do this. Each player should just go for it.
4. Put on relaxing music and do this activity quietly.
5. Encourage players to share their pictures with each other and see if they spark any thoughts or memories for the other players.

LET'S TALK ABOUT IT!

Was this relaxing, or were you antsy?

What can you do today to feel more like the right side of your paper?

DO YOU STACK UP?

ABOUT THE GAME

Kind self-talk can help a child feel brave and confident. Kids will use a fun relay race to practice saying nice things about themselves.

Game Materials
25 cups,
4 different-colored permanent markers,
4 pieces of paper

Time Needed
15 minutes

Who's Playing?
2 to 4 people

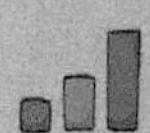

Difficulty
Level 2

Helpful Tips

For team play, make a set of cups and papers for each team and see who can finish first.

HOW TO PLAY

1. Write the following four phrases on four slips of paper using different colored markers for each:
   - I can do hard things.
   - I love myself no matter what.
   - I am kind.
   - I am strong.
2. Then, hide the papers around the room.
3. Use the four markers to place a different colored X on the bottom of each cup.
4. Instruct players to stack the cups into one pile, upside-down.
5. The first player observes the color of the X on the top cup and finds the slip of paper to match. When they find it, they can place the cup at the bottom of the stack.
6. Repeat until all slips are found.

LET'S TALK ABOUT IT!

What's something else you can practice saying to yourself?

THE TALLEST TOWER

ABOUT THE GAME

It is easy for children to get upset if they don't think they're good at something. This game will help children remember that every day is a learning opportunity, and it is great for working on patience.

Game Materials
15 craft sticks and 15 cups per team, markers

Time Needed
15 minutes

Who's Playing?
2 people per team

Difficulty
Level 2

Helpful Tip

Change the amount of time if the game is too easy or hard.

HOW TO PLAY

1. On the craft sticks, write the following phrases (five of each phrase):
   - I'm still learning to _____.
   - I'd like to learn _____.
   - Something I've learned to do is _____.
2. In teams of two, try to build a tower. Player 1 puts the first cup upside down on the floor.
3. Player 1 places a craft stick across the bottom of the cup and answers the question on the stick.
4. Player 2 puts another cup upside down on top of the craft stick and then another stick on top. Player 2 then answers the question.
5. Take turns, with the goal being to see how tall each team can build their tower in 5 minutes.

LET'S TALK ABOUT IT!

How many cups did you think you could stack?

Did it get easier?

WHY, THANK YOU, GOOD SIR!

ABOUT THE GAME

Compliments help build confidence. This game will help players practice giving and receiving compliments based on personalities, not just looks.

Game Materials
Poster board, markers, tape, rubber bands

Time Needed
20 minutes

Who's Playing?
2 to 5 people

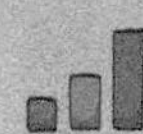

Difficulty
Level 2

Helpful Tip

If the task is too difficult, move closer to the target or use a foam dart gun.

HOW TO PLAY

1. Draw a target with three circles on the poster board.
2. In the center, write "You." In the middle circle, write "Give." In the outer circle, write "Ask."
3. Mark the starting line on the floor with tape.
4. Player 1 shoots a rubber band at the target. If a participant hits the center, instruct them to say something they like about themselves. Then, they get 3 points. Subsequently, if the player hits the middle circle, they give someone else a compliment and receive 2 points. If the player hits the outer circle, they ask someone to give them a compliment and receive 1 point.
5. Players take turns until someone gets 15 points.

LET'S TALK ABOUT IT!

What compliments make you feel good?

Are there any compliments that make you uncomfortable?

IT'S ALL GOOD

ABOUT THE GAME

A personality trait can be both a strength and a challenge. This game challenges personality traits to help kids think about how their various traits can be positive.

Game Materials
Index cards or paper, pens or markers, timer

Time Needed
15 minutes

Who's Playing?
4 or more people

Difficulty
Level 3

Helpful Tips

If needed, explain the words to the player giving the clues.

HOW TO PLAY

1. Write down the following word pairs below, each on a separate card or piece of paper. Put them in a pile facedown.
    - Bossy/Leader
    - Arrogant/Confident
    - Impulsive/Decisive
    - Hyper/Energetic
    - Make up more of your own!
2. Divide into two teams.
3. Player 1 from Team 1 picks a card and describes the word pair they pulled to the team.
4. Team 1 guesses the word pair. They earn 1 point for each correct word guessed (earning up to 2 points). Their turn is over if the team guesses both words, or after 2 minutes has passed.
5. Alternate teams and players for 15 minutes. The team with the most points wins!

LET'S TALK ABOUT IT!

What traits do you like about yourself but sometimes cause problems?

BE HEADSTRONG

ABOUT THE GAME

A reminder that practice can make things better can help a child have a good attitude about trying new things. With this game, participants will practice staying positive while using a tennis ball inside pantyhose to knock over cups.

Game Materials
Plastic cups, tennis ball or roll of socks (1 per player), pair of pantyhose (1 per player), timer

Time Needed
20 minutes

Who's Playing?
1 to 6 people

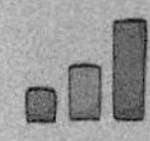

Difficulty
Level 3

Helpful Tip

Add cups or increase time as needed, and consider dividing up into teams.

HOW TO PLAY

1. Place 6 to 10 cups upside down on the floor throughout the room.
2. Each player places a tennis ball or roll of socks into one of the toes of the pantyhose.
3. The player then puts the large end of the pantyhose on their head like a headband.
4. The goal is to try to knock over the cups with the tennis ball without using their hands.
5. A player's turn is complete when all cups have been knocked over or when 2 minutes has passed.
6. Give everyone an opportunity and then add up the score of cups knocked down to determine the winner. Repeat if time allows to see if scores get better with practice.

LET'S TALK ABOUT IT!

Is there anything else in your life that will get easier with practice?

SHALL WE DUEL?

ABOUT THE GAME

It can be easy for kids to pay too much attention to negative things. Use this playing card challenge to give children practice letting go of negative thoughts and thinking more good ones.

Game Materials
Paper, playing cards, masking tape

Time Needed
20 minutes

Who's Playing?
2 to 4 people

Difficulty
Level 3

Helpful Tips

If time is limited, use face cards from the deck instead of drawing characters.

If there is an odd number of players, have someone "host" the duel.

HOW TO PLAY

1. Give each player a piece of paper the size of a card to draw their character. Line them up on the table. Mark a finish line 10 card lengths away using tape.
2. Put the playing cards in one stack face-down. Flip over the top card. The first player will guess if the next card will be higher or lower.
3. If correct, move forward a card length. If not, move backward.
4. If a player moves forward, they name a worry to let go of and take a deep breath. If a player moves backward, they place their hands on the table and name a positive thought.
5. Take turns until someone reaches the finish line to win the duel.

LET'S TALK ABOUT IT!

Do you think negative thoughts are ever helpful?

CHAPTER THREE

Discovering Ways to Communicate

Communication is how people connect with each other. People communicate in many ways: by using words, facial expressions, and body language. Communicating thoughts and feelings can be hard, but these games will help children learn and practice how to express themselves in healthy ways. Once children learn these skills, they'll be able to express themselves more clearly, let others know that they're listening, ask for help, and more. Kids can also learn communication skills from people around them, so it is important for adults to join in on the fun. These games will work even better if you model a good example.

COPYCAT

ABOUT THE GAME

Giving clear directions can be harder than it seems. In this activity, players will build something out of blocks and give directions to their partner to see if they can make a copy of the creation without seeing it.

Game Materials
Building blocks

Time Needed
10 minutes

Who's Playing?
2 people

Difficulty
Level 1

Helpful Tip

Encourage players to communicate by asking for help if needed, confirming when they understand a direction or completed a step, and so on.

HOW TO PLAY

1. Have one of the players pick out 15 building blocks. The other player then collects an identical set of blocks with the same number, types, and shapes.
2. Players then sit back-to-back, each with their set of blocks in front of them. Pick one of the players to go first.
3. Player 1 assembles a creation with their blocks.
4. Once their creation is complete, they will give directions to Player 2 so that they can attempt to construct an identical creation. Player 2 can ask questions if they are confused.
5. When Player 2 is finished, both players turn around and compare their builds.
6. Players then switch roles and repeat.

LET'S TALK ABOUT IT!

What might've made the directions easier to follow?

AYE, AYE, I-STATEMENTS

ABOUT THE GAME

I-statements are a great way to help children express how they are feeling. They say first what they're feeling, then what makes them feel that way, and last why. In this game, players will pop balloons and see if they can piece together I-statements.

Game Materials
Balloons, paper, pens or markers

Time Needed
15 minutes

Who's Playing?
2 or more people

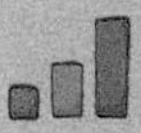

Difficulty
Level 1

Helpful Tip

For I-statements, the first part should name a feeling. The second part should describe what caused the feeling *without* blaming someone else. The third part should describe the effect of the situation.

HOW TO PLAY

1. Have each player write down several three-part I-statements, about five per player. Write down each part of the I-statement on a separate piece of paper. (For example: *I feel frustrated . . . when it's loud after dinner . . . because it's hard to focus on my homework.*)
2. Put each piece of paper in a separate balloon, blow it up, and tie it.
3. Have players take turns stomping on balloons to pop them and collect the papers.
4. When all the balloons are popped, see who can make the most I-statements.
5. It's okay if they don't make sense if they have all three parts!

LET'S TALK ABOUT IT!

When could you use an I-statement to express how you're feeling?

PRESENT AND ACCOUNTED FOR

ABOUT THE GAME

Giving kids the opportunity to practice good communication will help them work better when they are part of a team. In this activity, players will practice coming up with a plan, communicating clearly, and working as a team while they wrap a box "one-handed" with a partner.

Game Materials
For each team: empty box, wrapping paper, scissors, tape, ribbon

Time Needed
15 minutes

Who's Playing?
2 or 4 people

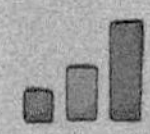

Difficulty
Level 1

Helpful Tip

Add "bonus time" to the clock for good teamwork if you're playing with just one team and they're not close to finishing.

HOW TO PLAY

1. Put players into pairs and give each team a set of materials.
2. Each player will put one arm behind their back, which they cannot use for the activity.
3. Each team must work together to wrap the box like a gift, covering the entire box.
4. After wrapping, the team must then wrap a ribbon around the box and tie a bow on top.
5. The first team to finish wins. If there is only one team, the players can race against a clock.

LET'S TALK ABOUT IT!

What parts were hard?

How did you work together?

How might you do better if you did this again?

PUCKER UP!

ABOUT THE GAME

Facial expressions can reveal a lot! Someone can show that they're mad or sad just by the look on their face. Players can use this game to practice paying attention to facial expressions to guess what food someone is eating.

Game Materials
For each player: slices of lemon, lime, orange, and other fruits; cup; paper and pencil

Time Needed
10 minutes

Who's Playing?
3 to 5 people

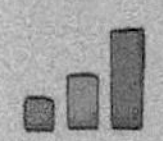

Difficulty
Level 2

Helpful Tip

Include at least one sour food for fun, and make sure no one has food allergies!

HOW TO PLAY

1. Provide precut slices of each fruit in a cup, concealing the types of fruits from the other players.
2. Using paper and pencil, each player writes down the players' names in one column and the foods in a second column.
3. All players close their eyes, put the food in their mouth, and then open their eyes.
4. Each player then uses their own paper and pencil to match the player to their food based on the facial expressions made by the other players.
5. The player with the most correct answers wins.

LET'S TALK ABOUT IT!

What other things can you tell from someone's facial expressions in real life?

SCAVENGER HUNT

ABOUT THE GAME

In communication, listening is just as important as talking. This activity is a scavenger hunt that players will do blindfolded with a partner giving directions. The goal is to give clear directions and listen closely to find all the items.

Game Materials
Paper, pen, blindfold

Time Needed
10 minutes

Who's Playing?
2 people

Difficulty
Level 2

Helpful Tips

Make sure players are comfortable with being blind-folded or closing their eyes.

If you have a larger group, this activity is fun for teams as well!

HOW TO PLAY

1. Pick someone to be the leader. The leader will make a list of items around the room that the other player or team will have to find. Items can be something specific like a pencil or a category like "something stretchy."
2. The other player will be blindfolded. The leader will give directions to help them find the items. For example, find:
   - Something soft
   - Something you could use to write with
   - Something white
   - Something that starts with the letter "S"
3. Set a timer for 5 minutes and see how many items you can find as a team. If playing individually, race the clock.
4. Switch roles and repeat the activity.

LET'S TALK ABOUT IT!

Do you prefer to be a leader or a teammate?

What would you do if both people wanted to be the leader?

STOP AND THINK

ABOUT THE GAME

When it comes to thinking before talking, patience and excitement can be a challenging mix for young minds. Here's a way to practice both.

Game Materials
Index cards, pencils, cup, dice

Time Needed
15 to 20 minutes

Who's Playing?
2 to 5 people

Difficulty
Level 2

Helpful Tip

Allow time so players can share as much as they would like.

HOW TO PLAY

1. Ask players to sit in a circle. Give each player five index cards and a pencil.
2. Instruct players to write four questions to learn more about the other players, each on a separate card. On the fifth card, write "SWITCH."
3. Players fold their cards in half and put them into the cup.
4. Player 1 picks a card from the cup and rolls the dice. If a player picks the "SWITCH" card, players jump up and switch places.
5. Player 1 answers the question using the number of words rolled. For example, if the question is "What was your most embarrassing moment?" and the player rolled a 7, they could respond, "I fell on stage in a play."
6. The player to the right goes next.
7. Take turns until all players have gone.

LET'S TALK ABOUT IT!

Was it hard to focus on counting once you knew what you wanted to say?

COMMUNICATION MEMORY

ABOUT THE GAME

Assertive communication is polite but to the point. Aggressive communication is rude or bossy. Play this memory game and practice the healthiest way to communicate—assertively.

Game Materials
Index cards, colored markers

Time Needed
15 to 20 minutes

Who's Playing?
2 people

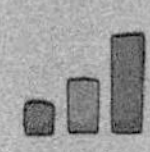

Difficulty
Level 2

Helpful Tip

Use a dictionary if you need help understanding the terms *passive*, *assertive*, and *aggressive* better.

HOW TO PLAY

1. On index cards, each player writes down 10 situations where they need to communicate—for example, "You want to invite a friend to a movie." or "You can't hear the teacher." Write three of the cards in blue, four in green, and three in red.
2. Make a second set of the cards with the same situations and colors.
3. Mix up the cards and put them facedown.
4. Players take turns flipping two cards to try to make a match.
5. If the cards match, the player keeps them. The player then acts out what they would say in the communication style that matches the color (blue = passive, green = assertive, red = aggressive).
6. When the cards are all matched, the player with the most matches wins.

LET'S TALK ABOUT IT!

How do you feel when people are being aggressive or passive?

GOING, GOING, GONE!

ABOUT THE GAME

Working as a team often means compromise or coming up with another way to decide on a plan. Practice teamwork and creativity to launch a ping-pong ball with limited supplies.

Game Materials
Scissors, cup, balloons, paper, paperclips, chopsticks, craft sticks, rubber bands, ping-pong balls

Time Needed
15 minutes

Who's Playing?
2 or 4 people

Difficulty
Level 3

Helpful Tip

For a harder challenge, try a golf or tennis ball.

HOW TO PLAY

1. Make teams of two.
2. Give each team an assortment of materials (the same materials to each team).
3. Give players 5 to 10 minutes to make a contraption that will launch (not strike) the ball as far as possible.
4. Players cannot throw the ball and cannot touch the ball other than to set up the contraption.
5. Players can touch the contraption to launch the ball, but they can't use one of the items to hit the ball. For example, players can pull the rubber band back and let it go to launch the ball, but they can't hit the ball with a chopstick.
6. See whose ball goes the farthest!

LET'S TALK ABOUT IT!

Did you agree on a plan?

Did you choose one player's plan, or did you compromise?

SAY WHAT?

ABOUT THE GAME

Open-ended questions help a conversation to keep going. They often start with one of the five Ws: *who, what, where, when,* or *why*. Practice using open-ended questions in this role-play conversation game.

Game Materials
Paper, pens, cup

Time Needed
15 to 20 minutes

Who's Playing?
3 to 5 people

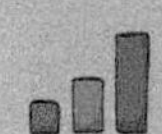

Difficulty
Level 3

Helpful Tip

To help players remember the five Ws, someone can write them down and put them in the middle of the circle.

HOW TO PLAY

1. Using a piece of paper, each player writes down an imaginary character. For example, a player could write "an alien that always gets lost" or "a dog who wishes he was a squirrel." Put players' papers in the cup.
2. Have players sit in a circle.
3. Player 1 picks a character from the cup and introduces themselves to the group (answers the *who* question).
4. Player 2 asks Player 1 a *what* question.
5. Players continue asking questions in order of the five Ws in "About the Game."
6. After five questions are answered, Player 2 picks a new character, and the group continues around the circle asking questions.

LET'S TALK ABOUT IT!

Is it hard to remember to ask people questions in real life?

When could you practice open-ended questions?

SPEAKING MY LANGUAGE

ABOUT THE GAME

Nonverbal communication means people communicate in ways other than using words. This activity will educate kids about body language.

Game Materials
Per player: index cards, pens or markers, 3 to 5 magazines, scissors, envelope

Time Needed
20 minutes

Who's Playing?
3 to 5 people

Difficulty
Level 3

Helpful Tip

Choose magazines with lots of photos of people.

HOW TO PLAY

1. On the index cards, have each player write down two phrases that could be expressed through facial expressions or body language—for example, "I'm nervous" or "I have so much energy!"
2. Place the index cards facedown and mix them up.
3. Player 1 picks a card. This player turns around while the others have 2 minutes to use magazines to find a person whose body language matches the card.
4. Each player cuts out their photo. Put all players' cutouts into an envelope.
5. Player 1 chooses the best match. The player who cut out the best match gets a point.
6. The player to the right picks the next card.
7. Play until all cards are gone. The player with the most points wins.

LET'S TALK ABOUT IT!

Can you think of a time when you noticed someone's body language and it was helpful?

CHAPTER FOUR

Soothing Stressful Moments

Stressful times happen throughout life. Stress can come from worries about school or from life changes like divorce or a new sibling. Sometimes stress can help people stay focused or try their hardest, but too much stress can make people feel sad, tired, or even sick. The challenges in these games can help children learn skills to deal with stress, such as taking a break, asking for help, or problem-solving. Learning how to handle stress when kids are young will give them a skill that they can use all through life. As always, the best way for adults to teach stress management is to be an example, so join in!

TO SOLVE OR NOT TO SOLVE

ABOUT THE GAME

Problems cause stress, but figuring out which problems can be solved takes practice. Use this sorting game to practice deciding when to solve a problem, when to ignore it, and when to ask for help.

Game Materials
8 sheets of paper,
2 pens, 2 scissors,
2 straws

Time Needed
15 minutes

Who's Playing?
2 people

Difficulty
Level 1

Helpful Tip

If time is limited, an adult can write down the problems before the activity.

HOW TO PLAY

1. Cut a sheet of paper into 2-by-2-inch squares.
2. Using the squares, each player writes down six problems, one on each square. For example, "Spilled orange juice on shirt."
3. Give each player three sheets of paper that will be the solution pages. Write "Solve it" on one, "Ask for help" on the second, and "Ignore it" on the third. Put them across the room.
4. On the command of "Go!" players will use straws to move the problem squares to the solution page that they think is the best fit. To do so, they will need to inhale to pick up a square and exhale to release it. No using hands!

LET'S TALK ABOUT IT!

What types of things should you always tell an adult?

EGG-SPLORING CONTROL

ABOUT THE GAME

Part of working through stress is understanding what can be controlled and what can't. This game will practice when to expend their energy and when to let go.

Game Materials
Eggs, spoons, buckets, permanent markers

Time Needed
20 minutes

Who's Playing?
2 to 6 people

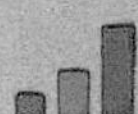

Difficulty
Level 1

Helpful Tip

You can choose any stressful situation for this game, such as divorce, moving, and so on.

HOW TO PLAY

1. Make two-player teams and give each team a dozen raw eggs.
2. On their eggs, have each team work together to carefully write down six things in their control and six things outside their control. For example, they control how much they study, but they can't control the noise in the classroom. Place the eggs in a bucket.
3. Have players take their eggs and spoons outside! Place two empty buckets per team 20 feet away from one another.
4. Label one bucket "IN" and one "OUT."
5. Players work in relay format to take turns loading an egg from the bucket on the spoon and carrying it to the "IN" or "OUT" bucket without breaking it. Have players exchange the spoon after each attempt.
6. The team with the fewest unbroken eggs wins!

LET'S TALK ABOUT IT!

How does it feel when something is out of your control?

TIC-TAC-TACKLE IT

ABOUT THE GAME

It's easy to get frustrated when problems pop up. It can help kids to remember that they've solved problems in the past. Use this ring toss tic-tac-toe game to talk about times that they've problem-solved.

Game Materials
9 soda bottles, index cards, pipe cleaners of two colors

Time Needed
15 minutes

Who's Playing?
2 people

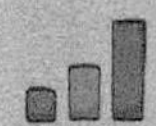

Difficulty
Level 1

Helpful Tips

You can use empty bottles and add rice for weight so they don't fall over.

Use glow bracelets for rings.

HOW TO PLAY

1. Set up the bottles in a three-by-three grid like a tic-tac-toe board.
2. On index cards, write the following:
   - At home
   - At school
   - With friends
3. Put a card at the top of each column.
4. Make five pipe cleaner rings for each player in a different color.
5. Players take turns tossing rings, trying to make three in a row like tic-tac-toe.
6. If a player lands a ring on a bottle, they are asked to describe a time they handled a problem that matches the card at the top of the column.
7. The first player to make three in a row wins. (Sometimes it'll be a tie!)

LET'S TALK ABOUT IT!

How does it feel before you solve a problem? After?

FREYA SAYS

ABOUT THE GAME

When something scary happens, the body reacts. It wants to fight, to run away ("flight"), or to freeze. It's the body's way of trying to keep a person safe. Play this version of Simon Says to help children remember and understand the three responses.

Game Materials
None

Time Needed
10 minutes

Who's Playing?
3 or more people

Difficulty
Level 1

Helpful Tip

The "fawn" response is another possible response. If you know about it, add it into the game, too.

HOW TO PLAY

1. Explain the fight, flight, or freeze responses to stress.
2. Pick a player to be the leader. The leader says, "Freya says fight," "Freya says fly," or "Freya says freeze."
3. For "fight," the other players will punch and kick the air. For "fly," they can fly or run in place. For "freeze," they should strike a pose.
4. The leader should occasionally give a direction without saying "Freya says," and the players should *ignore* the directions.
5. If a player makes a mistake, they are out. The last player wins and becomes the new Freya.

LET'S TALK ABOUT IT!

Have you ever had one of these responses to a stressful situation?

Could these responses ever cause a problem?

BUDDY-BUDDY BINGO

ABOUT THE GAME

This version of Bingo will help kids decide what qualities make a good friend and think about what makes friends special.

Game Materials
Paper, pencils, crayons or markers, scissors, cup

Time Needed
20 minutes

Who's Playing?
2 or more people

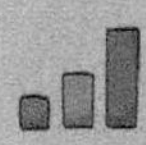
Difficulty
Level 2

Helpful Tips

Suggestions for friendship qualities include "stands up for me," "includes me in activities," "is honest with me," and so on.

HOW TO PLAY

1. Each player is given two sheets of paper and asked to draw a five-by-five grid on each. Have them color the middle square on one of the sheets. The other sheet should be cut into small squares.
2. Have the group come up with 24 qualities of healthy friendships while each player writes them randomly in the squares on their page.
3. Write each of the 24 qualities on separate slips of paper and put them in the cup.
4. Players take turns pulling a slip from the cup and reading it to the group while each player uses their squares to cover the matching spot on their paper and thinking about a friend who has that quality.
5. The first player to cover five spots in a row yells, "Buddy Bingo!"

LET'S TALK ABOUT IT!

What can you do if a friend does something that isn't very friend-like?

AND THEN?

ABOUT THE GAME

It's important for kids to learn that when problems pop up, it's okay to feel sad or annoyed at first. It can help a child to learn to focus on solving the problem though. Use this activity to practice problem solving and storytelling.

Game Materials
Timer, dice

Time Needed
10 minutes

Who's Playing?
3 or more people

Difficulty
Level 2

Helpful Tip

Write down the directions and post where the players can see them.

HOW TO PLAY

1. Sit in a circle. Have someone start telling a story with one sentence. Set a timer for 3 minutes.
2. The next player rolls one of the dice. The player then adds one sentence to the story, using the matching number to decide what happens. If you rolled:
    1. Things get better
    2. Things get worse
    3. Solves a problem
    4. Everyone, put hands on the floor or lap (Whoever is last takes the next turn)
    5. Everyone stands up, turns around, sits back down (Whoever is last takes the next turn)
    6. Any sentence!
3. Play continues until the timer goes off. The next player ends the story.

LET'S TALK ABOUT IT!

Was it easier to imagine ways that the story could get better or ways that it could get worse?

UNDER PRESSURE

ABOUT THE GAME

Learning to notice stress is a skill that will help kids know when they need to take more time to take care of themselves. This activity is good practice for helping with the challenge.

Game Materials
Painter's tape or chalk, 6 cups for each player, marshmallows, timer, chopsticks

Time Needed
10 to 15 minutes

Who's Playing?
1 or more people

Difficulty
Level 2

Helpful Tip

Be mindful of people's personal space when making the outlines of bodies. Some people may not be comfortable with help.

HOW TO PLAY

1. Using painter's tape or chalk, players trace an outline of their bodies on the floor.
2. Discuss ways stress can affect the physical body. This could look like a stomachache, or dizziness. Ask players to place a cup near the part of their body where they experience this.
3. Fill a separate cup with marshmallows.
4. Set a timer for 3 minutes.
5. Using only chopsticks, players transfer marshmallows to the cups where they feel stress. Ask them to notice which part, and cup, has the most marshmallows. If additional players are playing, ask if anyone can share a similar experience.

LET'S TALK ABOUT IT!

What helps when you experience feeling these things?

BULLY B-BALL

ABOUT THE GAME

Being the victim of bullying can be very scary. It can be stressful just to witness bullying. Use this game to encourage talking about bullying while playing basketball.

Game Materials
Paper cups, stapler or hot glue, cardboard box, ping-pong balls, scissors

Time Needed
20 minutes

Who's Playing?
1 or more people

Difficulty
Level 3

Helpful Tips

Write the meaning of the baskets where everyone can see.

Play as teams or race against a clock.

HOW TO PLAY

1. Cut the bottom off three paper cups. Staple or glue the bottomless cups onto the side of the box.
2. Write 1, 2, or 3 over each hoop.
3. Player 1 has 2 minutes to score as many baskets as possible. Players should bounce the ball on the table and then into the basket. Each basket is one point. If the player gets baskets in all 3 hoops, they score 5 bonus points.
4. To get the point, when a player scores a basket, they must give an example for the matching hoop:
    1. An example of bullying
    2. What you can do about bullying
    3. Effects of bullying

LET'S TALK ABOUT IT!

When should you talk to an adult?

What is cyberbullying?

ACTING OUT

ABOUT THE GAME

Friends can be a great help in handling stress. Use this game of charades to share things that have caused stress but also to come up with new coping skills.

Game Materials
Paper, scissors, pencils, cup, timer

Time Needed
15 to 20 minutes

Who's Playing?
4 to 6 people

Difficulty
Level 3

Helpful Tip

Before writing down the charades, remind players that their answers will be shared and not to write down anything that they'd like to keep private.

HOW TO PLAY

1. Cut paper into about 1-inch-by-4-inch slips
2. Each player takes 4 slips of paper, writes down two things that cause them stress and two things that they do to feel better, folds them, and then puts them in the cup.
3. Players take turns picking a piece of paper and acting it out for the rest of the group to guess.
4. Players can't talk, hum, sing, or make any noises. They *can* use props from the room.
5. Set a timer for 3 minutes for each player's turn.
6. If you think the actor is acting out your suggestion, don't spoil it for the rest of the group!

LET'S TALK ABOUT IT!

Were there any coping skills or stressors that you have in common with other players?

SMASH YOUR STRESS

ABOUT THE GAME

Physical activity can help reduce stress. It can also help to know that everyone deals with stress. In this activity, players can throw things and make a mess while talking about what is causing them stress.

Game Materials
Poster board, various colors of paint, cups, plastic wrap, plastic gloves

Time Needed
20 minutes

Who's Playing?
1 to 3 people

Difficulty
Level 3

Helpful Tips

Remind everyone beforehand to wear clothes that can get messy. Outside is best!

If you don't have gloves, use finger paint instead of acrylics, or fling paint from a paintbrush.

HOW TO PLAY

1. For each player, affix a poster board to a surface that can be covered in paint.
2. Pour a bit of each color paint into each cup.
3. Each player names something that causes them stress while making a small ball of plastic wrap and dipping it into the paint of their choice. Players can use gloves if they choose.
4. Players then throw the plastic wrap ball at the poster board, releasing their stress.
5. Repeat as many times as players like. Reuse plastic wrap balls if they don't stick to the poster board.

LET'S TALK ABOUT IT!

What stress is out of your control?

What is within your control?

What problems require help from an adult?

CHAPTER FIVE

Calming Angry Feelings

Angry feelings are common feelings to have. They can appear with hurt feelings or when something doesn't go as planned. It's easy to respond to anger by yelling, throwing something, or wanting to be alone. However, none of these responses will help solve the problem. They only avoid it. Learning ways to manage anger can help kids make better choices. The games in this chapter will help children learn ways to notice their anger, describe how they're feeling, and help calm down.

SHAKE, RATTLE, AND ROLL

ABOUT THE GAME

When kids feel angry, sometimes moving their bodies can help them feel less angry. Use this activity to get the feelings unstuck while shaking ping-pong balls out of a box.

Game Materials
12 ping-pong balls, marker, empty tissue box, ruler, scissors, belt

Time Needed
15 minutes

Who's Playing?
1 or more people

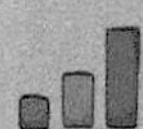

Difficulty
Level 1

Helpful Tip

Try it with a partner or group and see who can do it fastest!

HOW TO PLAY

1. As a group, have players think about 12 things that make them angry and write them on the ping-pong balls.
2. Cut the opening of the tissue box to 3 × 5 inches.
3. Make a small slit at the bottom left and bottom right edges of the box and push the belt through the left slit, across the inside of the box, and out through the right slit. It should look like the tissue box is a giant belt buckle!
4. One at a time, players buckle the belt around their waist and put the 12 ping-pong balls inside the tissue box.
5. Take turns seeing how quickly they can shake out the ping-pong balls without using their hands.

LET'S TALK ABOUT IT!

Can you think of other ways that moving your body has helped you calm down?

CALM THE STORM

ABOUT THE GAME

Anger quickly clouds the brain from being able to think properly. To think clearly, there is a need to calm the brain. Make a glitter jar to help kids learn to calm their angry feelings so they can make good choices.

Game Materials
9-ounce bottle of clear glue, 32-ounce mason jar, glitter of various colors, warm water

Time Needed
15 minutes

Who's Playing?
1 person

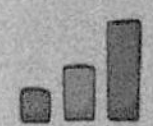

Difficulty
Level 1

Helpful Tip

Try using more than one size of glitter if you can. It will make the jar extra pretty.

HOW TO PLAY

1. Pour the bottle of glue into the jar, reserving a small amount for step 4.
2. Add about 4 spoonfuls of glitter.
3. Fill the jar ½ inch from the top with warm water.
4. Add a thin layer of glue around the inside of the top of the jar.
5. Close the jar tightly.
6. Shake!
7. Place the jar in a special place. When feeling angry, shake it, and wait to see if there is a sense of calm by the time the glitter settles to the bottom of the jar.

LET'S TALK ABOUT IT!

When the jar is "shaken up," it isn't clear. Is there a time that you couldn't think clearly because you were angry?

STOMP OUT ANGER

ABOUT THE GAME

Healthy coping skills are things that kids can learn to help them handle hard feelings. This activity helps players identify coping skills with the use of balloons while engaging in some popping of them along the way!

Game Materials
Paper, scissors, pens or pencils, 12 balloons per player, timer

Time Needed
15 minutes

Who's Playing?
2 to 4 people

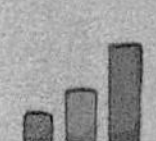

Difficulty
Level 1

Helpful Tip

Make sure the balloons are large enough that they aren't too difficult to pop.

HOW TO PLAY

1. Cut paper into thin strips, and have each player write down six coping skills for anger: things that help them calm down, things they can do if they need a break, or people who can help them if they become angry.
2. Have players place the six coping skill strips of paper and six blank strips in individual balloons, blow them up, and tie them.
3. Spread the balloons out across the ground.
4. Set a timer for 2 minutes.
5. Have players stomp on the balloons and try to pop them.
6. Players try to collect as many coping skills as possible before the timer goes off.
7. Have players take turns reading what they collected.

LET'S TALK ABOUT IT!

Can you think of times when you've used any of these coping skills?

SCRATCH THAT

ABOUT THE GAME

Sometimes anger hides a deeper emotion, like sadness, hurt, or fear. Once kids are calm, it's important for them to think about what else is felt. This activity will remind kids to scratch off the top layer to see what else is there.

Game Materials
Watercolor paper (1 per player), paintbrushes (2 per player), oil pastels, dish soap, black acrylic paint, hair dryer, quarter (1 per player)

Time Needed
20 minutes

Who's Playing?
1 or more people

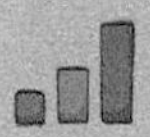

Difficulty
Level 1

Helpful Tip

Don't put the paint on too thick or it will take a long time to dry.

HOW TO PLAY

1. Give each player a paper and two brushes.
2. Instruct players to cover their paper with oil pastels in whatever colors they'd like. Have them brush off any crumbs when they're finished.
3. Mix 2 tablespoons of dish soap with 2 tablespoons of black paint.
4. Instruct players to paint a thin layer of black paint over their paper.
5. Let dry. Use a hair dryer to dry faster. (Air drying will take 20 to 30 minutes, so the activity may need to be done over two sessions.)
6. Have players use a quarter to scratch the black paint, revealing color underneath, and draw whatever they desire.

LET'S TALK ABOUT IT!

Have you acted angry when you had another feeling underneath?

FISHING FOR FEELINGS

ABOUT THE GAME

Sometimes people act angry when they have another feeling inside. For example, someone might act mean when they feel jealous or embarrassed. See how feelings might not match behavior with this fishing game.

Game Materials
Hot glue, 4-foot-long piece of string (1 per player), round disc magnets (1 per player), large box, pens or markers, index cards (5 per player), large paper clips (5 per player)

Time Needed
20 minutes

Who's Playing?
2 or more people

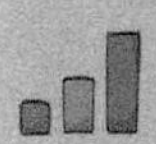
Difficulty
Level 2

Helpful Tip

Challenge players to put the string on a stick and stand away from the box.

HOW TO PLAY

1. Have each player hot glue a magnet to the end of a piece of string.
2. On the outside of the box, as a group, write down 10 ways that people might act if they are angry.
3. When someone is angry, they may have other negative feelings that people can't see (like jealousy or disappointment). Have each player write five of those feelings on separate index cards.
4. Have players fold the index cards in half and put a paperclip on the folded edge.
5. Have each player hold the empty end of the string and use the magnet on the other end to fish out a feeling card. Continue until all cards are removed.

LET'S TALK ABOUT IT!

Have you ever acted angry, but once you were calm, you noticed another feeling?

ANGRY ANIMAL

ABOUT THE GAME

Anger can make kids feel like they want to hit or punch someone. Instead, find something that a child can hit or punch safely, like play dough. Encourage players to make an angry animal and see if their partner can name it.

Game Materials
4 to 5 containers of play dough

Time Needed
15 minutes

Who's Playing?
2 people

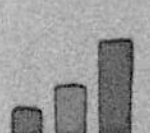
Difficulty
Level 2

Helpful Tip

Try using self-drying clay instead and keep the animals.

HOW TO PLAY

1. Players take time to think of an animal that acts like they feel when they're angry. Does it hide? Does it attack? Does it eat too much? Players should keep their choice to themselves and not tell their partner what animal they've picked.
2. Give players 5 minutes to make their animal out of play dough.
3. After 5 minutes, players have three guesses to see if they can guess what the other player has made.
4. Players are encouraged to share what made them pick that animal and how it is like them when they're angry.

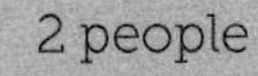

LET'S TALK ABOUT IT!

How do people react to you when you're angry?

Does it help you feel better? If not, what would?

DON'T BURST MY BUBBLE

ABOUT THE GAME

It can be hard not to react quickly when angry, but taking a breath before reacting will help kids make a better choice. Give them an opportunity to practice impulse control by moving a bubble with their breath.

Game Materials
Wire hanger,
1 container of bubbles (containing 1 bubble wand)

Time Needed
10 minutes

Who's Playing?
2 or more people

Difficulty
Level 2

Helpful Tip

A hula hoop is a good replacement for the hanger.

HOW TO PLAY

1. Pull the bottom of a hanger to make the opening wider. Bend the opening into a circular shape (as much as possible).
2. Have one player stand on the opposite side of the room or, if outside, about 15 feet away, holding the hanger up like the Statue of Liberty holding her torch.
3. Opposite the player holding the hanger, have players stand and take turns blowing a bubble and trying to direct the bubble through the opening of the hanger using only their breath.
4. Players can work as a team to blow the bubble toward and through the hanger.

LET'S TALK ABOUT IT!

How hard was it to keep control if you got excited?

Do you breathe faster when you're angry? Do you hold your breath?

3, 2, 1, MARSHMALLOW

ABOUT THE GAME

When frustrated, kids can use coping skills to help calm down. In this game, players will stack marshmallows while using a coping skill to match their frustration level.

Game Materials
Large marshmallows, chopsticks (1 set per player), timer

Time Needed
10 minutes

Who's Playing?
2 or more people

Difficulty
Level 3

Helpful Tip

If an adult participates, they can model positive self-talk by talking to themselves, saying things like "Just take it slow and do your best."

HOW TO PLAY

1. Using only chopsticks, stack as many marshmallows as possible in 5 minutes.
2. As participants play, they will use numbers to describe how frustrated they are. The number "1" means they feel fine. The number "2" means they are a little frustrated, and "3" means they are *very* frustrated.
3. Assign a "Freezemaster" to yell "Freeze" about every 45 seconds, and have each player state the number that describes their level of frustration.
4. If players are a 1, they don't need to do anything. If they're a 2, they should take a deep breath and exhale slowly. If they're a 3, they should take a deep breath, exhale slowly, and wiggle or stretch.
5. After 10 seconds, the Freezemaster will tell everyone to start again.

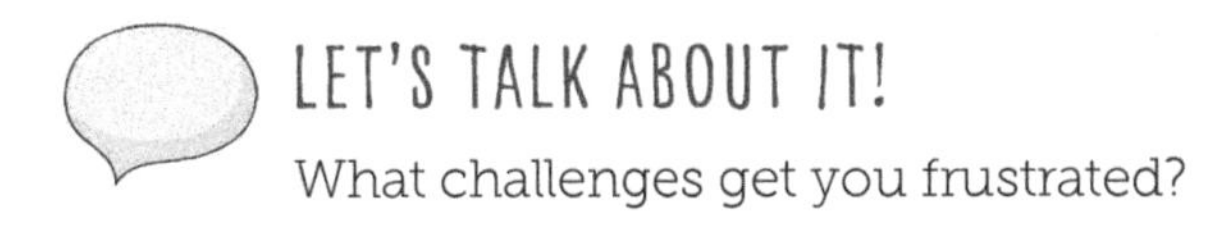

LET'S TALK ABOUT IT!

What challenges get you frustrated?

BREAK DOWN

ABOUT THE GAME

When kids get angry, they can find it hard to control their words and behaviors. Through this activity, by trying to collect marbles on top of a cup, they can practice stopping even when they might not want to.

Game Materials
For each player: pint glass, tissues, rubber band, sink, pencil, marbles

Time Needed
20 minutes

Who's Playing?
2 or more people

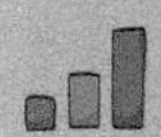

Difficulty
Level 3

Helpful Tip

If someone's tissue breaks, put on a new one for the next turn.

HOW TO PLAY

1. Have each player cover a glass with a tissue and secure it with a rubber band.
2. Gently run the top of each glass under water until the tissue covering the top of the glass is completely wet. Poke a small hole in the center of the tissue with a pencil.
3. Players then try to put as many marbles as possible on top of the jar without the tissue breaking.
4. Players can stop adding marbles whenever they want and get a point for each marble that safely stays atop the jar. If the tissue breaks, no points are awarded.
5. Each player gets three attempts. Add up the points; the player with the most points wins.

LET'S TALK ABOUT IT!

How do you know when you need to take a break from something frustrating?

FOUR IN A ROW

ABOUT THE GAME

It's easy to stay in feelings of anger rather than talking about ways to solve the problem. Here, children use a fun activity to practice talking about their anger.

Game Materials
3 egg cartons, scissors, tape, 1-inch fuzzy pom-poms in at least two colors, permanent marker

Time Needed
20 minutes

Who's Playing?
2 people

Difficulty
Level 3

Helpful Tips

For a challenge, bounce colored ping-pong balls instead.

HOW TO PLAY

1. Cut the tops off egg cartons. Tape the bottoms together to make a 6 × 6 grid and number each column 1 to 6. Place the egg carton creation on the floor.
2. Have each player take turns throwing their set of pom-poms.
3. Players respond to the following based on what row a pom-pom is in:
    - Name another word for *angry*.
    - Describe a time when you handled anger well.
    - Describe a time when you wish you handled your anger differently.
    - Name a person who helps calm you when you're angry.
    - Name something you can do to help calm down.
4. The first player to get four in a row horizontally, vertically, or diagonally wins.

LET'S TALK ABOUT IT!

The next time you get angry, what could you do to make the situation easier to manage?

AN
XIE
TY

CHAPTER SIX

Acknowledging Anxiety

Anxiety is often thought of as a bad thing, but anxiety is the body's attempt to stay safe. However, the body sometimes gets confused. Sometimes it will try to protect itself when it is already safe. When someone is anxious, people might be tempted to say things like "Don't worry" or "It's not a big deal." Trying to talk someone out of their anxiety or telling them to ignore it altogether doesn't work. To soothe anxiety, there is a need to put the fear into words, talk back to negative thoughts, and soothe the body's physical reaction. This chapter will provide playful ways for kids to learn these skills.

AND A CHERRY ON TOP

ABOUT THE GAME

Gratefulness helps the mind stay positive and experience less stress. Gratefulness means to be thankful for the good things in life. This activity will show players how to notice the good things in their lives.

Game Materials
Cups, whipped cream, timer, bag of small candy-coated chocolates

Time Needed
10 minutes

Who's Playing?
1 or more people

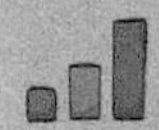

Difficulty
Level 1

Helpful Tip

Make sure no one has food allergies and let everyone eat their creations!

HOW TO PLAY

1. Fill a cup per player or team with whipped cream above the brim of the cup.
2. Set a timer for 5 minutes.
3. Players throw candies one at a time, trying to get them to stick to the whipped cream.
4. Each time a player throws a candy, they are encouraged to name something that makes them feel grateful.
5. The goal is to see how many candies each player can get into their cup.
6. The player or team with the most candies stuck onto the whipped cream at the end of the 5 minutes wins.

LET'S TALK ABOUT IT!

How does your body feel when you think of positive things?

Was it easy or hard to think of things?

UNWRAP ANXIETY

ABOUT THE GAME

Anxiety can be helpful to get started on a task or to study for a test, but sometimes it gets in the way and distracts when trying to focus. Have kids use this unwrapping challenge to take notice of how pressure affects them.

Game Materials
10 large clothing/costume items, 2 boxes, wrapping paper, tape, four oven mitts

Time Needed
20 minutes

Who's Playing?
2 or 4 people

Difficulty
Level 1

Helpful Tips

For a greater challenge, use clear packing tape instead of Scotch tape.

HOW TO PLAY

1. Before the game, wrap five clothing/costume items in each box. Try to find silly items.
2. Have each player put oven mitts on both hands.
3. Give each player a wrapped box.
4. Each player must unwrap and open their box and put on all the clothing items without taking off the mitts.
5. The first to finish is the winner.
6. If playing with four people, make teams of two. Have one player open the box and the other player put on the clothes.

LET'S TALK ABOUT IT!

Oven mitts keep us safe, but they cause problems when they are used at the wrong time. Anxiety is the same. When could it be helpful?

TWO FEARS AND A LIE

ABOUT THE GAME

Anxiety can affect people differently. Something what worries one person might not worry someone else. Talking about fears can make them less scary. Use this guessing game to give kids practice talking about their fears.

Helpful Tip

Younger players might have a hard time coming up with a realistic "lie." Feel free to help.

HOW TO PLAY

1. Have players sit in a circle.
2. Have Player 1 name two things that cause them anxiety and one that does not. When choosing something that does *not* cause anxiety, try to choose something that *could* cause someone else anxiety. When telling the three things to the group, the player is free to mix them up in whatever order they'd like.
3. Take turns having the other players try to guess which one of the fears is a lie. Give a point for every correct guess.
4. If nobody guesses, Player 1 tells the group which one of the fears is a lie and no points are awarded.
5. Repeat until everyone has a turn.

LET'S TALK ABOUT IT!

Did you have any fears in common with others?

STAND TALL

ABOUT THE GAME

When children are scared, it's important they know how to name the feeling and discuss it with a trusted adult. Give kids practice naming scary things and voicing *how* scary they are with this tower-building game.

Game Materials
Construction paper, scissors, markers, stapler, timer

Time Needed
15 to 20 minutes

Who's Playing?
2 to 5 people

Difficulty
Level 2

Helpful Tip

If there is an adult who isn't participating, they can be the Freezemaster and cut the strips of paper beforehand.

HOW TO PLAY

1. Have each player cut construction paper into 20 1-inch strips along the short side.
2. Encourage players to write something that scares them on each slip.
3. Staple the ends of each strip together, forming individual rings.
4. Choose one player to be the "Freezemaster."
5. Individually or in teams, stack the rings, forming a tower.
6. Periodically, the Freezemaster will yell, "Freeze!"
7. Each player/team will look at what is written on the top ring of their tower. Ask each child to rank their scare on a scale of 1 to 5, with 5 being the scariest.
8. Continue for 7 minutes and see how many rings players can stack.

LET'S TALK ABOUT IT!

Did you notice anything happening in your body?

AMYGDA-WHAT?

ABOUT THE GAME

The amygdala is the part of the brain that acts like a guard dog. It must be calm for the brain to be able to think or remember things. Use this puzzle activity to help kids remember how the brain works.

Game Materials
Picture of a dog, box, 8-inch paper circle, picture of a brain (1 per team), scissors, tennis ball

Time Needed
15 minutes

Who's Playing?
1 to 4 people

Difficulty
Level 2

Helpful Tip

If you want to play in teams of two, you can have one player roll the ball and one player complete the puzzle.

HOW TO PLAY

1. Put the picture of the dog on the front of a box. On the floor in front of the box, put an 8-inch paper circle.
2. For each team, cut the picture of the brain into 10 puzzle-like pieces and put them in a pile.
3. From 5 feet away, take turns having teams roll the ball onto the circle in front of the dog. This "helps the dog calm down." Keep trying until someone on the team is successful.
4. Next, each team must work together to complete the brain puzzle.
5. The first team to do both first wins.

LET'S TALK ABOUT IT!

Did the frustration or pressure make it harder to focus?

CUP O' CALM

ABOUT THE GAME

Cortisol is a chemical that gives the body energy when it thinks it is not safe. Too much can make the body tired or sick though. Use this game to remind kids why it's important to find "calm."

Game Materials
20 cups per player, paper, scissors, 2 straws, markers, paper

Time Needed
15 minutes

Who's Playing?
2 people

Difficulty
Level 2

Helpful Tip

To add to the learning potential, draw the chemical symbol for cortisol on the papers.

HOW TO PLAY

1. Before starting the game, on the inside bottom of the cups, write one of the letters C, A, L, or M. Make five of each.
2. Put three 1-inch squares of paper inside the cups, covering the letters inside.
3. Have players use straws to remove the paper from the cups by inhaling and pulling each piece out of the cup until they can see the letter.
4. If they uncover a letter and already have that letter, they discard it face up on the table. The other team can steal it.
5. The first player to collect all the letters to spell "CALM" wins.

LET'S TALK ABOUT IT!

When might your body have a lot of cortisol?

How can you help your body calm down and decrease cortisol?

SUMMON YOUR SUPERHERO

ABOUT THE GAME

Standing like a superhero can help the brain feel more confident. To do it, have players stand up with their fists on their hips, their feet shoulder width apart, and their shoulders back and head up. Practice with this card game.

Game Materials
2 decks of playing cards

Time Needed
20 minutes

Who's Playing?
3 to 5 people

Difficulty
Level 3

Helpful Tip

When someone puts down a joker, try to make the other players laugh by making silly faces.

HOW TO PLAY

1. Pull out cards numbered 2 to 5, face cards (not aces), and jokers.
2. Shuffle and deal the cards into a facedown pile.
3. Player 1 flips a card, puts it in the middle, and says, "Two." Player 2 flips over a card and says, "Three." Players continue through five and then go back to two.
4. If the word matches the number, everyone puts their hand on top of the card in the middle. The last player takes the card.
5. On a king or queen, everyone jumps into superhero pose. The last player takes the card.
6. On a joker, be totally quiet. Whoever makes a noise first takes the card.
7. The first player to get rid of their cards wins.

LET'S TALK ABOUT IT!

How does it feel when you stand like a superhero?

BUT WHAT IF?

ABOUT THE GAME

When anxious, the brain will focus on mostly bad things. Kids can be taught to change their thoughts by practicing countering with negative thoughts. Consider using this tumbling tower game to have them learn some ways to do it.

Game Materials
Tumbling tower, marker, paper

Time Needed
20 minutes

Who's Playing?
2 to 4 people

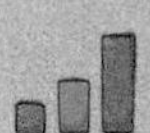

Difficulty
Level 3

Helpful Tip

To make the pieces easier to find, write the number on both ends.

HOW TO PLAY

1. Using a tumbling tower, write the numbers 1 to 6 on the ends of the blocks.
2. On a sheet of paper, write:
   - Will that matter in a year?
   - How likely is this?
   - Could someone help me?
   - Could something good happen instead?
   - Is there proof that this will happen?
   - Is there a solution?
3. Build the tower.
4. Player 1 begins by naming a worry, saying, "What if ______?" and then picks a numbered question from the list and answers.
5. Player 1 removes the corresponding numbered piece from the tower and places it on top of the tower.
6. Take turns until the tower falls.

LET'S TALK ABOUT IT!

Are there any worries that you have where this might help?

OVER IT

ABOUT THE GAME

Sometimes a child may be overloaded with worries and their body needs rest. That's why it is important to teach them to notice when they need a break or help. Use this water game to give them practice thinking about it.

Game Materials
32-ounce mason jar, gallon jug of water, cake pan, cups (1 per player), dice

Time Needed
15 minutes

Who's Playing?
2 to 4 people

Difficulty
Level 3

Helpful Tip

Use any size cups and jar. Just change the amount of water in cups and the jar based on their sizes.

HOW TO PLAY

1. Fill the jar halfway with water and put it inside the cake pan.
2. Have each player fill their cup with about 2 inches of water.
3. Player 1 rolls a die. If the number rolled is even, they pour some water from their cup into the jar and name something that causes them anxiety. If the number is odd, they name something that makes them feel better and use the jar to fill their cup with 1 more inch of water.
4. If a player's cup becomes empty, add water from the gallon jug.
5. Players continue taking turns until the jar overflows.

LET'S TALK ABOUT IT!

How do you know when you're close to overflowing?

KNOCK, KNOCK IT DOWN

ABOUT THE GAME

Children can often shy away from telling someone how they're feeling. This game will help kids practice using their words to share their feelings.

Game Materials
11 cups, paper, scissors, pens or markers, ball (or crumpled paper)

Time Needed
10 minutes

Who's Playing?
2 people

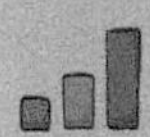

Difficulty
Level 3

Helpful Tip

Swap out the words or use the game for a different type of feeling.

HOW TO PLAY

1. Stack 10 cups into a pyramid, either on the floor or a table, 10 to 12 feet away from the players.
2. Make two sets of the following words on slips of paper: *worried*, *nervous*, *scared*, *anxious*. Put them in the remaining cup along with four blank slips. This is the "feeling jar" and should be placed near the players.
3. Talk about the words as a group and make sure everyone knows the meanings.
4. Players take turns throwing the ball at the pyramid.
5. If a player knocks a cup down, they pick a slip out of the feeling jar and describe a (real or made-up) time when they had that feeling. They should try saying, "I felt ____ when ____."
6. Repeat until all cups are toppled. Reset, if necessary, to include everyone.

LET'S TALK ABOUT IT!

What other words describe anxiety?

CHAPTER SEVEN

Sitting with Sadness

Being sad sometimes is a normal part of life. Sadness can happen after a big change, like moving to a new house or parents getting divorced. It's okay to be sad, and it's okay to cry, too. Going through sad times and feeling sad feelings isn't fun, but it's important for kids to understand to let themselves have the sad feeling. Sometimes feeling sad might be over quickly, and sometimes it might last for a long time. The activities in this chapter will help kids explore sad feelings and see what they can do to feel better.

ANIMAL YOGA

ABOUT THE GAME

When a child feels sad, they may sometimes think it's a good idea to hide it or pretend they're okay, which doesn't actually help. Using this yoga activity to teach them to stretch and move their bodies can be beneficial.

Game Materials
None

Time Needed
10 to 15 minutes

Who's Playing?
2 or more people

Difficulty
Level 1

Helpful Tip

Some people are nervous being the center of attention. If it's more comfortable, lead in pairs.

HOW TO PLAY

1. Have players stand in a circle and pick someone to go first.
2. Player 1 thinks of an animal, and without telling the group, strikes a pose that best shows what animal they're imagining. When choosing a pose, players should try to pick a pose that helps them stretch.
3. Player 1 continues the pose and encourages everyone to copy them. They should hold the pose for 30 seconds while taking and releasing deep, relaxing breaths.
4. After 30 seconds, see if group members can guess what animal Player 1 picked.
5. The player to the right will go next. Go around the circle until everyone has a turn, or go around a second time if it is a small group.

LET'S TALK ABOUT IT!

How do you feel after taking time to move and breathe?

BOUNCE BACK

ABOUT THE GAME

Sometimes sadness comes from things that are out of a child's control. Sometimes it comes from a problem that they can solve. Use this bouncy ball challenge to help children remember and think about the difference.

Game Materials
Empty trash can,
2 bouncy balls (about 1 inch wide)

Time Needed
10 minutes

Who's Playing?
1 or more people

Difficulty
Level 1

Helpful Tips

You can play with a group if there's enough space. It works best on hard floors!

HOW TO PLAY

1. Make sure there is nothing around that can break easily.
2. Put the trash can against a wall.
3. Have players stand 10 feet away from the trash can and bounce the first ball on the floor as hard as they can. The first ball represents sadness that slows down over time.
4. While that ball bounces, have the player quickly move three steps toward the trash can and see if they can bounce the second ball on the floor and into the trash can before the first ball stops bouncing. The second ball represents sadness that they have some control over.

LET'S TALK ABOUT IT!

When was a time that you solved the problem that caused your sadness?

When did you just have to wait?

MIX IT UP

ABOUT THE GAME

Feelings can be overwhelming when kids experience more than one big feeling at the same time. Help a child think about mixed feelings with this art activity by mixing up colors and making pretty, marbleized paper.

Game Materials
Baking tray, shaving cream, food dye in several colors, spoon, white cardstock, ruler

Time Needed
20 minutes

Who's Playing?
1 person

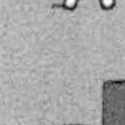

Difficulty
Level 1

Helpful Tip

Scrape off the top layer of shaving cream and repeat the activity with fresh colors.

HOW TO PLAY

1. Fill the baking tray with a thin layer of shaving cream.
2. Have the player think of a time when they felt sad. Have them also try to think of any other feelings they had at the same time.
3. Instruct the player to put drops of different colors in the shaving cream, representing each of their feelings.
4. Have them use the spoon to swirl the colors around. They can add more drops and swirl again if they'd like.
5. Encourage the player to press the cardstock into the shaving cream.
6. Guide the player to slowly remove the cardstock and scrape off the shaving cream using the ruler.
7. Place the paper somewhere safe to dry.

LET'S TALK ABOUT IT!

When have you had more than one feeling?

FIND THE ENDORPHINS

ABOUT THE GAME

Endorphins are chemicals that produce the sensation of happiness. The body makes endorphins when someone laughs, cries, exercises, or snuggles with their pet. This game will look for ways to make the brains and bodies feel good.

Game Materials
Bag of multicolored pom-poms, paper, pencils, timer

Time Needed
5 minutes

Who's Playing?
2 people

Difficulty
Level 1

Helpful Tip

Instead of pom-poms, you could use an item like a stuffed animal.

HOW TO PLAY

1. Have players work as a team to write down five activities that help them feel better, a minimum of one for each color of pom-pom, and write the color of the pom-pom on the paper.
2. Player 1 then closes their eyes while Player 2 hides the pom-poms paired with the papers listing the feel-good activity.
3. Set a timer for 5 minutes.
4. Player 1 attempts to find all the pom-poms in 5 minutes. When pom-poms are found, Player 1 shakes the pom-pom with excitement while reading the activity written on the paper.
5. Other player(s) can give clues by "happier" if they're close or "sadder" if they're not close.
6. Switch roles and play again.

LET'S TALK ABOUT IT!

Have you ever noticed feeling better after doing a specific activity?

STRUT YOUR STUFF

ABOUT THE GAME

Combine coping skills and get twice the mood boost! This game helps kids move their bodies and listen to fun music to make them feel better physically and mentally. Pick a DJ and get dancing!

Game Materials
Music player,
2 beanbags

Time Needed
10 minutes

Who's Playing?
3 people

Difficulty
Level 1

Helpful Tip

If beanbags are not available, put beans or rice in a sealable sandwich bag. Tape it closed to be safe.

HOW TO PLAY

1. Players pick a fun, upbeat song.
2. One player (the DJ) oversees the music. Other players go to one side of the room and put a beanbag on top of their head.
3. The DJ turns on the music. Players try to dance their way across the room.
4. When the DJ pauses the music, players must freeze.
5. When the DJ turns the music back on, players begin to dance and walk again.
6. Players must go back to the starting line if their beanbag falls off or if they stop dancing without the DJ pausing the music.
7. The first player to cross the room becomes the new DJ.

LET'S TALK ABOUT IT!

Do you have any favorite dance songs that make you feel good?

COZY CORNER

ABOUT THE GAME

The space around a child can affect how they feel. In this challenge, players will draw a cozy space that would help someone who's feeling sad. They will then see if they can "pin" themselves into the cozy corner.

Game Materials
Poster board, markers, tape, smiley stickers

Time Needed
20 minutes

Who's Playing?
2 people

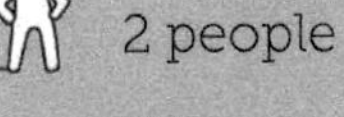

Difficulty
Level 2

Helpful Tip

Take as many turns as you want and use a blindfold if you'd like.

HOW TO PLAY

1. Ask players to imagine they're feeling sad and want to relax in their bedroom.
2. On a poster board, draw the most relaxing room they can imagine. Encourage players to think of each sense (sight, smell, touch, sound, and taste) and include anything that would help them feel cozy.
3. Affix the poster board to a wall.
4. Play begins with Player 1 standing 10 feet away from the poster board with their eyes closed, holding a smiley sticker.
5. Player 1 spins quickly in a circle three times and then moves toward the poster board, attempting to place the sticker closest to their safe space in their bedroom.
6. Player 2 repeats the activity.
7. See who can get closest.

LET'S TALK ABOUT IT!

What do you have at home that helps you feel better if you're sad?

FLIPPY FEELINGS

ABOUT THE GAME

Knowing the words to use to talk about feelings can make it easier to do. In this activity, players will work as a team to spell out four words for *sad* while engaging in a flip-a-cup challenge.

Helpful Tip

Make a second set of cups if you want to include more people and make it a competition.

HOW TO PLAY

1. On the outside bottom of each cup, write one letter, spelling out the following words:
   - Lonely
   - Jealous
   - Guilty
   - Hurt
2. Randomly stack the cups and place half of the stack on a table in front of each player.
3. Simultaneously, players remove a cup from the top of their stack and place it bottom down, slightly overhanging the edge of the table.
4. Players use one finger to flip the cup by striking the overhanging portion so that the cup lands upside down on the table. Repeat until successful.
5. When all cups have been flipped, the players work to unscramble and arrange the cups to spell all four words for *sad*.

LET'S TALK ABOUT IT!

Do you know other words that describe sadness?

TUNE IN

ABOUT THE GAME

Music is a mood changer that can be used to change kids' moods if they're feeling down. In this activity, kids will make a playlist of songs to help them feel better.

Game Materials
Computer (or phone or tablet), paper, pencil

Time Needed
20 minutes

Who's Playing?
1 person

Difficulty
Level 2

Helpful Tip

Use parental controls if a child is using a device on their own.

HOW TO PLAY

1. With an adult's permission, the player will use a computer, tablet, or phone to search for "happy" or "feel-good" songs.
2. As the player searches for songs, encourage them to listen to as many as they can in the time given.
3. The player is encouraged to write down the names of songs that they like that help them feel positive and energetic.
4. The goal is to create a playlist of at least 10 songs.
5. After creating the playlist, have the player write down a list of times and circumstances when it could be helpful to listen to "happy music."

LET'S TALK ABOUT IT!

It's okay to be sad sometimes. What are the signs that it's time to try to feel better?

IN THE CLOUD

ABOUT THE GAME

When children are feeling bad, it can help to remind them that feelings pass with time, like clouds in the sky. You can help them practice focusing on this idea and breathing through it with this cloud-making experiment.

Game Materials
Jar with lid, ⅓ cup very warm water, aerosol hairspray, 5 ice cubes

Time Needed
5 minutes

Who's Playing?
1 person

Difficulty
Level 3

Helpful Tip

Have an adult pour the water if it's too hard.

HOW TO PLAY

1. Pour the water into the jar and secure the lid.
2. Place the ice cubes on the jar lid.
3. Wait about 30 seconds; then remove the ice cubes and lid.
4. Spray the hairspray into the jar for 2 seconds.
5. Quickly put the lid back on the jar and the ice cubes back on top of the lid.
6. Have the player watch a cloud form inside the jar while thinking of something that is making them feel sad or made them sad in the past.
7. Open the jar, and have the player take a deep breath (not of the escaping air), and imagine the sad feeling passing as the cloud disappears.

LET'S TALK ABOUT IT!

What helps you feel better when you're sad?

SNACK ATTACK

ABOUT THE GAME

In this activity, use snack time to encourage communication and support among peers.

Game Materials
8 ounces of room-temperature store-bought pizza dough, knife, flour, pizza sauce, 2 spoons, shredded cheese, pizza toppings, baking sheet, oven, potholders, pizza cutter, 2 plates, napkins

Time Needed
20 minutes

Who's Playing?
2 people

Difficulty
Level 3

Helpful Tip

If time allows, work as a team and make a full-size pizza!

HOW TO PLAY

1. Players wash their hands. On a clean work surface, cut the dough in half. Give each player one dough half.
2. Mold the piece of dough into a 6-inch circle. Say this piece of dough represents them. Use flour as needed to work the dough.
3. Players cover the middle of their dough with two spoonfuls of sauce. Explain that it represents sadness.
4. Remind players that they can rest and feel sad. Each player adds shredded cheese to their pizza.
5. Offer additional toppings to players and encourage them to name something that helps them feel better for each one added.
6. Place the pizzas on a baking sheet, and bake them in a 475-degree oven for 12 minutes or until the crust is light brown.
7. Once the pizzas have cooled, ask the kids to enjoy their snack with their baking partner.

LET'S TALK ABOUT IT!

What did you learn about your partner?

CHAPTER EIGHT

Creating a Bully-Free Zone

Bullying is when a person tries to be hurtful toward another person repeatedly. Stopping bullying is important because it can cause serious problems. When a person is bullied, they might feel sad, avoid school, have stomachaches, or even try to hurt themselves. This chapter will teach children ways to make spaces safe and kind, to notice and understand bullying, and to stand up to bullying. Knowing how to handle bullying will help kids be more confident and will help keep them and their friends safe.

COMPLIMENTAR-TREE

ABOUT THE GAME

Being kind to others can feel good. It also helps create an attitude of kindness so that people know bullying isn't welcome. Use this tree-making activity to practice kindness.

Game Materials
Poster board, markers, construction paper, scissors, glue

Time Needed
20 minutes

Who's Playing?
4 people

Difficulty
Level 1

Helpful Tip

Include as many people as possible. Cut out smaller leaves instead of hands if it is a large group.

HOW TO PLAY

1. Work as a group to draw a tree trunk on the poster board.
2. Have each player trace their hand six times on whatever color paper they would like and cut them out.
3. On each paper hand, have players write six compliments, two compliments for each of the other three people in the group. Remind players to compliment personality and ability, not simply the way someone looks.
4. Have players glue the hands onto the poster board as if they were leaves. They can be on the tree or in the wind, and some may have fallen to the ground.
5. Players can also draw branches and any background that they'd like.

LET'S TALK ABOUT IT!

How does it feel to get compliments?

What is a compliment that you would like to receive?

SO SORRY

ABOUT THE GAME

This fun sorting challenge will help kids learn the parts of a good apology so that they'll have the right words when they need them.

Game Materials
Markers, paper, scissors, 8 oranges

Time Needed
20 minutes

Who's Playing?
2 people

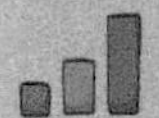

Difficulty
Level 1

Helpful Tip

Write down the order of steps where players can see.

HOW TO PLAY

1. Give each player a marker, piece of paper, and scissors.
2. Have each player write the following steps to apologize on their piece of paper:
    - Admit what you did.
    - Explain why it was wrong.
    - Say what you'll try do next time instead.
    - Ask if there's anything else you can do.
3. Each player then cuts the steps into separate slips of paper and places them randomly across the floor, writing side up.
4. Each player is given four oranges and labels them 1 through 4. Place them on the floor across the room slightly apart from each other.
5. Each paper gets on their knees, and then using only their knees (no hands!), move numbered oranges onto their paper slips to demonstrate how to apologize.
6. The first player to complete the task wins.

LET'S TALK ABOUT IT!

What would you do if someone doesn't accept your apology?

ALLY BRACELETS

ABOUT THE GAME

One way to prevent bullying is to let bullies know that it isn't cool or funny. In this activity, kids will make a bracelet to show that they're welcoming to new people and that they'll stand up against bullies.

Game Materials
Pony beads, stretchy clear string, beads with letters

Time Needed
15 minutes

Who's Playing?
2 people

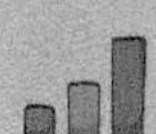

Difficulty
Level 1

Helpful Tip

Tape one end of the string to the table while you put on the beads.

HOW TO PLAY

1. Have each player choose a color for their bracelets. Players are encouraged to choose a color that people will notice and ask about to encourage conversation about bullying and acceptance.
2. Each player should chose a message to be placed on their bracelet. Examples include "Sit with us," "Bully Free Zone," and "BFZ" for short.
3. While discussing what their message will be and why, each player begins creating their bracelet using the colored and letter beads to spell their unique message.
4. After the bracelets are completed, if time allows, encourage players to make extra bracelets for friends who agree to welcome people who need a friend.

LET'S TALK ABOUT IT!

How might you be able to tell if someone needs a friend or if they're being bullied?

KINDNESS ROCKS

ABOUT THE GAME

People might forget quickly when they've said something unkind to someone else, but the other person might remember it much longer and feel hurt. Use this rock-decorating activity to think about the power of words.

Game Materials
4 smooth rocks (large enough to write several words), pencils, paint, paintbrushes

Time Needed
20 minutes

Who's Playing?
2 people

Difficulty
Level 1

Helpful Tip

If there is time, make a kindness garden and plant flowers with the rocks.

HOW TO PLAY

1. Each player takes two rocks and uses a pencil to write something mean that has been said to them in the past on the rock.
2. Players are then encouraged to trade rocks with a partner and talk to them about how they felt when someone said the mean thing to them.
3. Over top of the mean message, have each participant paint something kind. Examples include "You are loved" and "You are smart."
4. Have each player also paint a separate kindness rock for their partner.
5. Find a special spot to put the rocks (with the kind side up). Take home the ones that your partner painted for you or display them together somewhere.

LET'S TALK ABOUT IT!

How did it feel to have someone say something kind?

CRACKING UP

ABOUT THE GAME

Standing up to bullies can be scary. Encourage kids to challenge themselves with this game to see how many ways they can come up with to keep an egg from breaking.

Game Materials
1 empty gallon milk jug, scissors, bag of cotton balls, egg

Time Needed
15 minutes

Who's Playing?
1 or more people

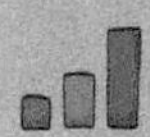

Difficulty
Level 2

Helpful Tip

If you have a group, see if everyone can come up with the ways of dealing with bullies without the list.

HOW TO PLAY

1. Carefully cut the top off a milk jug so that it creates a bowl about 5 inches high.
2. Aloud, read this list of ways to deal with a bully.
   - Walk away.
   - Tell an adult.
   - Tell them they're not being nice.
   - Be confident.
   - Stick with a friend or a group.
3. Have players add a total of five cotton balls to the bowl for each of the ways that were named.
4. If players can think of more ways, add five additional cotton balls for each.
5. Taking turns, have players drop the egg from 2 feet above the cotton-filled bowl and see if it cracks!

LET'S TALK ABOUT IT!

You can help prevent a messy situ-ation by knowing how to deal with bullies. What have you tried?

IT'S IN THE BAG

ABOUT THE GAME

It can be easy to forget that everyone's life is different. People deal with problems that they may never make known, like a learning challenge, difficult family life, or mental health issue. Use this building challenge to practice empathy.

Game Materials
Timer, mini plastic toy construction bricks, 2 gallon freezer bags

Time Needed
15 minutes

Who's Playing?
2 people

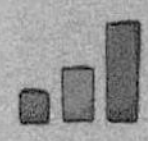

Difficulty
Level 2

Helpful Tip

Add other challenges, like having eyes closed or using one hand.

HOW TO PLAY

1. Set a timer for 5 minutes and encourage players to build whatever they would like with the plastic bricks.
2. When the timer goes off, have players explain their creation to each other.
3. Each player take a plastic bag and put four handfuls of plastic bricks into the bag.
4. Seal the bag with some air still inside, but make sure that players can grab individual bricks with their hands on the outside of the bag.
5. Set a timer for 5 minutes and encourage players to try to build the same thing that they built before.
6. When the timer goes off, have each player discuss their challenges with the activity.

LET'S TALK ABOUT IT!

What kind of things might someone be struggling with that you don't know about?

KINDNESS CHALLENGE

ABOUT THE GAME

A random act of kindness is when an act is done for someone with no expectation of anything in return. Encourage kids to try this challenge to spread kindness in their community.

Game Materials
Per player: calendar, pencil, paper

Time Needed
15 minutes

Who's Playing?
1 or more people

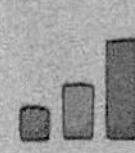

Difficulty
Level 2

Helpful Tip

Try to come up with as many ideas as you can that won't need any supplies.

HOW TO PLAY

1. Encourage players to think of 20 different acts of kindness they could do over the next month with at least one act of kindness in each of the following categories: give a small gift, donate something to charity, clean up a space in the community, compliment someone, write a letter expressing gratitude, do something good for the environment, do something nice for someone at school.
2. Give each player a calendar and a pencil and have them schedule days to implement their plan for kindness.
3. Have players make plans for a list of supplies they'll need to complete the acts of kindness.

LET'S TALK ABOUT IT!

Have you ever had someone do something nice for you as a surprise? How did it feel?

BULLY BUSTER

ABOUT THE GAME

Understanding why people bully can help kids come up with ways to prevent bullying or think of ways to respond to it. This activity will give kids practice by encouraging them to guess some of the reasons that bullies might bully.

Game Materials
Poster board, markers

Time Needed
15 minutes

Who's Playing?
3 people

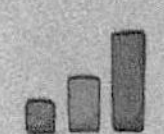

Difficulty
Level 3

Helpful Tip

Have an adult be the host. Add the option to "phone a grown-up" (the host) for a hint.

HOW TO PLAY

1. One player is assigned to be the host and holds the list of reasons that people might bully, but they don't let the group read the list.
   - They are jealous.
   - Someone has been mean to them.
   - They think it's cool.
   - They want to be funny.
   - They want attention.
2. The other two players take turns guessing what's on the list, writing their responses on the poster board.
3. For a guess that's not on the list, a player receives 1 point. For a guess that *is* on the list, a player receives 2 points.
4. The game is over when players have guessed all five reasons or when both players have had five turns.

LET'S TALK ABOUT IT!

Have you ever been tempted to be mean to someone for any of these reasons?

WHAT IS A BULLY?

ABOUT THE GAME

It's not always clear whether a behavior counts as bullying. Here, kids discuss what they think bullying is and see if their ideas match with a friend's.

Game Materials
Index cards, pencils

Time Needed
15 minutes

Who's Playing?
2 people

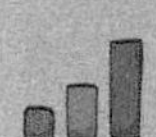

Difficulty
Level 3

Helpful Tip

Have an adult explain bullying if anyone is confused.

HOW TO PLAY

1. Each player writes down five examples of something that they believe is bullying on five separate cards. Then they write down five examples of something that might not be nice but isn't bullying.
2. Combine all players' cards together, mix them up, and put them in a stack facedown in the middle between the players.
3. Have each player write down "Bullying" on a new index card and "Not Bullying" on another card. Each player keeps the two cards in front of them.
4. Players take turns picking a card from the stack and reading it aloud.
5. Each player then holds up the card that they think matches with what was read ("Bullying" or "Not Bullying").
6. Encourage players to talk about why they think what they think.

LET'S TALK ABOUT IT!

Is it hard to be sure what counts as bullying?

ANTI-BULLYING CONTRACT

ABOUT THE GAME

One of the best ways to prevent bullying is to have a plan and to get friends to join kids in standing up to bullying. Use this activity to encourage kids to work together to come up with a plan and commit to it.

Game Materials
Paper, pencil

Time Needed
20 minutes

Who's Playing?
1 person

Difficulty
Level 3

Helpful Tip

If players have a hard time coming up with ideas, give some examples or assistance.

HOW TO PLAY

1. Use the questions in step 3 to come up with ways to prevent bullying, stand up to bullies, and help people who are being bullied.
2. Have players write down the sentences in step 3 and fill in the blanks. Players should write at least three ideas for each.
3. Player will read the contract with an adult to make sure the ideas are safe and then sign and date the contract.
   - I will look for bullying behaviors like ______.
   - If I see someone being bullied, I will ______.
   - I should ask for help from an adult if ______.
   - Adults who I can ask for help are ______.
   - I will make kindness cool by ______.

LET'S TALK ABOUT IT!

How do you feel about the ideas? Do they feel easy? Hard?

CHAPTER NINE

Feeling Safe in Your Skin

Sometimes in life, people experience scary things, like car accidents or even the death of a loved one. When this happens, it is normal to feel scared, unsafe, and unable to stop thinking about the scary thing, even after it is over. This is called trauma. Trauma can keep the body from feeling safe or calm, so it's important to work with a therapist. However, this chapter will give kids other ways to help them feel safe and confident.

ON YOUR FEET

ABOUT THE GAME

Grounding is an activity that can help kids focus on the present moment. It can be helpful if they're getting distracted by scary or negative thoughts. Give kids practice grounding with this guessing game in which they guess where they're standing.

Game Materials
4 disposable baking trays, rice, sand, small pile of leaves, cotton balls

Time Needed
15 minutes

Who's Playing?
2 people

Difficulty
Level 1

Helpful Tip

For extra messy fun, add a tray of gelatin or spaghetti.

HOW TO PLAY

1. One player leads the activity, and the other player is the guesser. The guesser should not see the supplies and should leave the room while the leader sets up.
2. The leader will fill each tray with a different material. Put enough material in the tray to completely cover the bottom.
3. The guesser will take off their shoes and socks and come back into the room with their eyes closed. The leader puts one of the trays in front of them and helps them to step into it.
4. The guesser will try to guess what is in the tray.
5. Take turns.

LET'S TALK ABOUT IT!

Are there any of the materials that you liked? Any that you disliked?

FOLLOW THE LEADER

ABOUT THE GAME

A key to feeling safe is knowing it's possible to say "no" during times that are uncomfortable or against the rules. This game will help children practice saying "no."

Helpful Tip

If there is a disagreement about what is safe, have players share their thoughts.

HOW TO PLAY

1. Pick a leader and have players line up behind them.
2. The leader walks around the room moving however they would like (waving arms, marching, etc.). Everyone follows and copies the leader.
3. As the leader walks, they'll ask the group to do something with them (for pretend). They could say, "Let's go to the movies!" or "Want to play basketball?"
4. The followers will yell, "OKAY!" and keep copying.
5. After three safe choices, the leader suggests something unsafe, like "Let's steal this gum." The group stops and yells, "NO WAY!"
6. The leader moves to the end of the line.
7. Repeat until everyone has been the leader.

LET'S TALK ABOUT IT!

Have you ever felt pressured by a friend to do something that you didn't want to do? How did that make you feel?

TRUST YOUR GUTS

ABOUT THE GAME

The body can give a person a "gut feeling" to help them know if they can trust someone and if they are safe. Sometimes gut feelings can be confused with simply feeling nervous. Give kids practice telling the difference using this messy toilet paper game.

Game Materials
Paper, markers, tape, play dough, cup of water

Time Needed
20 minutes

Who's Playing?
2 or more people

Difficulty
Level 2

Helpful Tip

This game is MESSY, so consider doing this activity outside.

HOW TO PLAY

1. Find an empty wall.
2. Have players write "Safe" on one piece of paper and "Not Safe" on a second piece of paper. Tape them on the wall 4 feet apart.
3. Player 1 will name a time they felt nervous but they were safe.
4. The player will then tear off 5 feet of toilet paper, wrap it into a loose ball, dip it half-way into the water, and throw it at the "Safe" sign.
5. The player will then name a time when they had a gut feeling about something and then make and throw a wet toilet paper ball at the "Not Safe" sign.
6. Repeat for all players

LET'S TALK ABOUT IT!

What should you do if you're having a gut feeling and you feel uncomfortable or unsafe?

IT'S A SECRET

ABOUT THE GAME

Some secrets are okay to keep, but not all. A good secret is exciting and can usually be shared later. A bad secret could end with someone getting hurt. Help kids decide which secrets are bad and knock them down.

Game Materials
2-inch-square sticky notes, pen, rubber band

Time Needed
15 minutes

Who's Playing?
1 person

Difficulty
Level 2

Helpful Tip

Have an adult join and lead a discussion at the end.

HOW TO PLAY

1. Take off a sticky note and put it so the sticky part is facing up and at the bottom.
2. Above the sticky part, have the player write down an imaginary secret. Repeat this step for 10 secrets: five secrets that would be okay to keep and five secrets that players should tell an adult.
3. Put the sticky part of the note against the side edge of a table so that the secret is showing. Line up all 10.
4. Set a timer for 5 minutes and have the player use the rubber band to attempt to shoot down all the bad secrets.

LET'S TALK ABOUT IT!

What should you do if you don't know if a secret is okay to keep?

SPACE INVADERS

ABOUT THE GAME

One way to help people feel safe is to give them space. Give kids experience with proper spacing by encouraging them to play this bubble-popping game and having them try to keep their distance from others.

Game Materials
Masking or painter's tape, bubbles

Time Needed
10 to 15 minutes

Who's Playing?
4 to 7 people

Difficulty
Level 2

Helpful Tip

If there is not enough space inside, use chalk to draw circles on a blacktop outside.

HOW TO PLAY

1. Use the tape to make a square on the floor for each player. The squares should be 3 feet across with 3 feet in between squares.
2. Players choose a square and stand inside. Pick a player to blow bubbles first.
3. That player should blow bubbles all around the room. They will name a body part that the players should use to pop the bubbles, such as "right hand" or "nose."
4. Players should pop the bubbles with that body part and cannot go outside their square. After 2 minutes, switch players. Continue until all players have a turn.

LET'S TALK ABOUT IT!

How do you feel when people get too close in real life? What can you do?

SHOUT IT OUT

ABOUT THE GAME

When something bad has happened, it is easy to replay it over and over. That's called ruminating. One way to stop it is to yell, "Stop!" Help kids decorate a pillow they can scream into when they are ruminating.

Game Materials
1-foot felt squares, fabric scissors, fiber fill, fabric markers

Time Needed
20 minutes

Who's Playing?
1 person

Difficulty
Level 3

Helpful Tip

Use light colors of felt so the markers will show up.

HOW TO PLAY

1. Take one piece of felt and cut it into a circle. Trace the circle on a second piece of felt and cut that out as well.
2. Put the circles on top of each other and cut from the edge toward the center, making a cut about 3 inches long. Continue cutting slits around the circle, making the slits about ½ inch wide.
3. With the circles still on top of each other, tie one strand to its matching strand underneath. Continue ¾ around the circle.
4. Fill the pouch with fiber fill. Then continue tying the remaining strands.
5. Decorate with fabric markers.

LET'S TALK ABOUT IT!

Have you ever had something stuck in your head and kept thinking about it even though you didn't want to?

INSIDE OR OUT?

ABOUT THE GAME

When something bad happens, it's helpful for children focus on what they can control and not blame themselves for things that are out of their control. This activity will give kids more practice with recognizing what's in their control, and what's not.

Game Materials
Paper, pens, timer

Time Needed
10 minutes

Who's Playing?
2 people

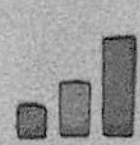

Difficulty
Level 3

Helpful Tip

Work together as a team or see who can come up with the most ideas.

HOW TO PLAY

1. As a group, choose a favorite fairy tale or movie. Then, as individual players, have each imagine that they're the main character.
2. Give each player a piece of paper and a pen.
3. Have each player draw a big circle in the middle of their page.
4. Set a timer for 5 minutes.
5. Each player is encouraged to write down things they can think of that were within the character's control inside the circle and write down things that were outside their control outside the circle.
6. After the time is up, share as a group.

LET'S TALK ABOUT IT!

Have you ever had something bad happen and you were tempted to give up?

What did you do instead?

Were you able to solve the problem?

SAY NO MORE

ABOUT THE GAME

Saying "no" can be hard, especially if someone doesn't accept "no" when it is said. This game will give kids more experience saying "no" through role play.

Game Materials
String, scissors, stapler, index cards, cup

Time Needed
15 minutes

Who's Playing?
2 people

Difficulty
Level 3

Helpful Tip

Encourage players to say their response like they would in real life.

HOW TO PLAY

1. Cut five pieces of string 3 feet long. Staple an index card to one end of each string.
2. Write each of the following statements on its own card:
   - "No thanks."
   - "You need to ask a parent."
   - "You should think about that first."
   - "I don't want to, but I hope you have a good time."
   - "How about doing something different?"
3. Poke a small hole in the bottom of the cup. Push string through the hole so that 3 inches of each string shows out the bottom.
4. Player 1 will role-play asking Player 2 to do something.
5. Player 2 will pull one of the ends of the string, see which response was pulled, and act it out. Continue taking turns.

LET'S TALK ABOUT IT!

What would you do if someone kept asking after you've already said "no"?

STRANGER DANGER

ABOUT THE GAME

It is normal to have different rules for family, close friends, acquaintances, and strangers. These rules are called boundaries. This game will teach children how to understand and implement boundaries.

Game Materials
Index cards, pencils, paper

Time Needed
10 minutes

Who's Playing?
4 people

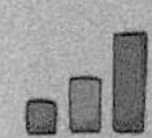

Difficulty
Level 3

Helpful Tip

Explain the difference between an acquaintance and a friend.

HOW TO PLAY

1. Grab 12 index cards. Write each of the following terms on three cards:
   - Family
   - Close friend
   - Acquaintance
   - Stranger
2. Each player privately takes one card.
3. Take 5 minutes to ask each other questions. Questions must be phrased, "Would you be comfortable if . . .?"
4. Players respond to questions as if they are the person on their card. Players can ask each other five questions. Answer questions with "yes," "no," or "maybe."
5. Have each player keep a piece of paper with them and write down who they think each person is.
6. After 5 minutes, see who got the most right.

LET'S TALK ABOUT IT!

Were there any questions that you were unsure how to answer?

TRAUMA OR NOT?

ABOUT THE GAME

Trauma is when something *very* scary or upsetting happens. Even after the scary thing is over, people might get very scared when something happens that reminds them of it. Give players the opportunity to determine what is trauma and what is not.

Game Materials
Paper, pencils

Time Needed
10 minutes

Who's Playing?
3 people

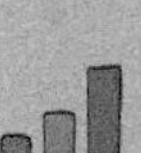

Difficulty
Level 3

Helpful Tip

This game is best if an adult can host. Add more examples if possible.

HOW TO PLAY

1. Pick one player to host the game. Only the host should read the directions.
2. Give each player a sheet of paper and a pencil.
3. Read this list of situations and ask players to write down which are traumas.
    - A car accident
    - A pet died
    - Someone's home is hit by a hurricane
    - Lost in the airport
    - Backpack stolen by bully
    - A friend doesn't keep a trusted secret
4. Once the players finish writing, read this: "There are no right or wrong answers. What is trauma to one person might not be to someone else. It depends on how the person feels."

LET'S TALK ABOUT IT!

If you have experienced something really scary, whom can you tell?

CHAPTER TEN

Marching On After Loss

Everyone will experience big and small losses at some point in their life. Grief is the natural and normal response to a difficult loss or change. A lot of people think that grief only happens when someone dies, but it can also happen over the loss of a friendship, due to divorce, or because of switching schools. Some ways to help with grief are to notice and accept the sadness, remember happy memories, and remember that hard feelings get easier over time. This chapter offers special tools for kids to use to better understand their feelings of grief.

CH-CH-CH-CHANGES

ABOUT THE GAME

When there are big changes in life, it is easy to feel all alone. However, it is likely that a child's friends have been through big changes, too. Play this game to see what changes kids have in common.

Game Materials
Paper, quarter

Time Needed
15 minutes

Who's Playing?
5 people

Difficulty
Level 1

Helpful Tip

Some ideas for changes are parents divorced, moved, changed schools, a pet died, a family member got sick, and so on.

HOW TO PLAY

1. Pick one player to host.
2. Put five pieces of paper on the floor, making a path across the room. Leave 3 feet in between each.
3. The players stand around the first square.
4. The host names a life change. (See the Helpful Tip for ideas.) If a player has been in that situation, they raise their hand.
5. The host then flips a quarter to decide how the players who raised their hands will move: They should go ahead one space if the quarter lands on heads and go back one space if it lands on tails.
6. The player who gets to the end first wins.

LET'S TALK ABOUT IT!

Did you have anything in common with people that you didn't know about before this game?

BUBBLE MEMORIES

ABOUT THE GAME

Even when people are gone, memories of them remain. People "leave a mark." Use this activity to remind kids that even though someone isn't with them anymore, the ways that they impacted them are still here.

Game Materials
Paper, scissors, 4 bowls (around 6 inches across), water, liquid dish soap, food dye, straws

Time Needed
20 minutes

Who's Playing?
2 people

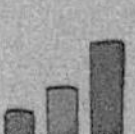

Difficulty
Level 1

Helpful Tips

Use cardstock or watercolor paper if possible.

Put down a plastic tablecloth for less mess.

HOW TO PLAY

1. Cut a piece of paper into a heart for each player
2. Fill the bowls with an inch of water and add 2 tablespoons of dish soap to each.
3. For each bowl, choose a color of food dye and add four drops.
4. Use a straw to blow bubbles in one of the bowls until they grow over the top of the bowl. Don't let them spill over onto the table.
5. Hold the heart over the bowl and lower the front of the paper onto the bubbles until they pop on the paper. Lift the paper.
6. Repeat with other colors until the heart is covered.
7. Let the paper dry.

LET'S TALK ABOUT IT!

What are your favorite memories of people who aren't with you anymore?

LIGHT UP THE ROOM

ABOUT THE GAME

Missing someone or something can feel sad, but there is comfort in thinking about good memories and making a cozy space. Use this activity to help kids make a memory jar that glows.

Game Materials
For each player: paper, scissors, pen, mason jar, glow-in-the-dark fabric paint, paintbrush

Time Needed
20 minutes

Who's Playing?
1 or more people

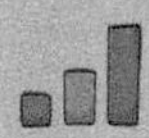

Difficulty
Level 1

Helpful Tip

Think of any kind of loss: divorce, a move, or changes after an illness or injury.

HOW TO PLAY

1. Have each player think of something or someone they miss.
2. Give each player a sheet of paper and have them cut the paper into 1-inch strips.
3. Encourage each player to write down 10 or more happy memories of the thing or person they miss on separate strips of paper.
4. Have each player put the strips inside a jar and put on the top.
5. Use the fabric paint to put small dots of paint on the outside of the jar. Leave a little bit of space between the dots so that the inside of the jar remains visible.
6. Let the jar dry and have players place it in a special spot near where they sleep to remind them of happy memories.

LET'S TALK ABOUT IT!

How does it feel to think happy memories about the person or thing that you miss?

PAST, PRESENT, AND FUTURE

ABOUT THE GAME

Think about how grief changes over time. Players will use colors to show how they felt, how they feel, and how they hope to feel in the future while painting rocks.

Game Materials
Bottles of acrylic paint of various colors, 6 smooth rocks (4 to 5 inches wide, 3 per player), plastic wrap

Time Needed
15 minutes

Who's Playing?
2 or more people

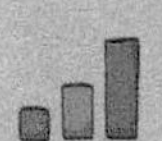

Difficulty
Level 1

Helpful Tip

Choose different colors for the different rocks.

HOW TO PLAY

1. Have players think of a big change in their life that was a loss. While they think about what life was like before the loss, players will pick out three or four colors of paint.
2. Each player will put 2 to 3 drops of paint (straight from the bottle) of each color onto the top of a rock.
3. Place a flat sheet of plastic wrap over the paint and squish it around until the top of the rock is covered with paint.
4. Repeat with a second rock, but have players imagine how they feel about the loss right now.
5. Repeat for the third rock, but have players imagine how they'd like to feel in the future.

LET'S TALK ABOUT IT!

Do you know anyone else who has had a big loss in their life?

LIVE IN TODAY

ABOUT THE GAME

While grief might not go away completely, it will become easier to know. Use this activity to help kids remember that it will get easier by writing a postcard from future them.

Game Materials
Cardstock, scissors, drawing materials

Time Needed
20 minutes

Who's Playing?
1 or more people

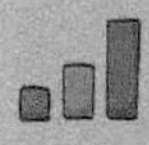
Difficulty
Level 2

Helpful Tip

If players are stuck, offer some ideas on what advice or encouragement the future them might offer.

HOW TO PLAY

1. Cut the cardstock into postcard-sized pieces and give each player one.
2. Instruct players to think about a loss or change that feels sad right now.
3. Ask them to create a postcard to send to that loss or change. On one side of the cardstock piece, ask children to draw a picture of it.
4. On the other side of the cardstock, instruct each player to write a note to the loss or change. The note should provide an update of how the child is doing right now, and any other news to share.

LET'S TALK ABOUT IT!

How likely does it seem that your wishes for the future will come true?

Is there anything you can do to make it more likely?

HOPPY HEART

ABOUT THE GAME

Sometimes grief sneaks up at unexpected times. When an event is a reminder of something upsetting, it's called a trigger. Use this activity to talk to kids about triggers.

Game Materials
3 cups water, ⅛ cup un-popped corn kernels, 32-ounce mason jar, 2 tablespoons baking soda, 6 tablespoons white vinegar

Time Needed
15 minutes

Who's Playing?
2 or more people

Difficulty
Level 2

Helpful Tip

For more fun, everyone can write down their guesses and share them after adding each ingredient.

HOW TO PLAY

1. Pour the water and the popcorn kernels into the jar.
2. Have players discuss what they think will happen when the baking soda is added to the jar.
3. Have a player add the baking soda and watch as a group to see what happens.
4. Have players discuss what they think will happen when the vinegar is added to the jar.
5. Have a player add the vinegar and watch as a group to see what happens.
6. As a group, discuss what the ingredient was that triggered something and what it affected.

LET'S TALK ABOUT IT!

Sometimes you won't know what will make you have a reaction. Have you ever had something unexpectedly remind you of someone you missed?

STEPPING-STONES

ABOUT THE GAME

Sometimes sadness can be so strong that it makes it hard to get through a normal day. Use this game to show kids how feeling sad can get easier with time.

Game Materials
Masking or painter's tape, brown and gray construction paper, scissors

Time Needed
15 minutes

Who's Playing?
1 or more people

Difficulty
Level 2

Helpful Tip

Work as a team and share rocks to cross the "river."

HOW TO PLAY

1. Use masking tape to make an X on the floor to show the starting point and an X to show the ending point. Place them as far away from each other as possible (25 feet, if possible).
2. Cut 20 pieces of paper into rock-like shapes (1 rock per sheet, 10 of each color).
3. Have players pretend that they're trying to cross a river that flows between the two X's.
4. Have each player name a happy memory (and receive a gray rock) or name something that helps them get through problems (and receive a brown rock).
5. Place them on the floor as stepping-stones and see how many rocks are needed to cross the river.

LET'S TALK ABOUT IT!

You may have days when you feel extra sad. What might cause those days?

LISTEN UP

ABOUT THE GAME

When someone passes on and leaves another person's life, it's challenging to put those feelings of grief and sadness into words. One way to alleviate that heaviness is to talk about the person who has passed. Encourage kids to use this game to share.

Game Materials
Paper, pencils

Time Needed
15 minutes

Who's Playing?
2 to 6 people

Difficulty
Level 2

Helpful Tips

If the loss is more recent, an adult should conduct the interview.

HOW TO PLAY

1. Ask players to pick a partner. Give each a piece of paper and a pencil.
2. Ask players to think of someone or something that they miss, such as a person or pet who has passed away, a friend who moved, or a parent who doesn't live with them anymore.
3. Instruct one partner to interview the other using the following questions. Write down the answers.
   - What was the person like?
   - When do you miss this person the most?
   - What is your favorite memory of them?
   - What do you do when you miss them?
4. Switch roles and repeat.
5. Share what you learned with the group.

LET'S TALK ABOUT IT!

How does it feel to talk about this person?

MISSION INVISIBLE

ABOUT THE GAME

Even when a loved one is no longer around, kids may still feel a heartfelt connection to them. This guessing game and obstacle course helps kids to imagine an invisible connection between two things.

Game Materials
Paper, scissors, bell

Time Needed
10 minutes

Who's Playing?
4 people

Difficulty
Level 3

Helpful Tip

When the player runs into lasers, they can be given a chance to guess what objects are connected.

HOW TO PLAY

1. Cut out two paper hearts.
2. Have one player leave the room.
3. The other players will choose two sets of objects that they will pretend are connected by a laser. For example, a player could choose to pretend the doorknob is connected to a light switch across the room.
4. Then the players will put the hearts on the floor to mark the start and end of the obstacle course.
5. Have the fourth player return to the room and stand on the starting heart.
6. The player then attempts to get to the end without running into "lasers." If the player hits a "laser," the other players will ring a bell.

LET'S TALK ABOUT IT!

Whom do you feel connected to even if you're not together?

PIECE IT TOGETHER

ABOUT THE GAME

When someone or something is very missed, a lot of feelings are possible all at once—anger, sadness, helplessness, fear, and even relief. This activity will remind kids that life is made up of all kinds of feelings and none of them are bad.

Game Materials
Colored construction paper, scissors, markers, glue

Time Needed
15 to 20 minutes

Who's Playing?
1 person

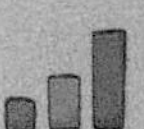

Difficulty
Level 3

Helpful Tip

You can glue the pieces word-side up, word-side down, or mixed up.

HOW TO PLAY

1. Cut 10 1-inch strips of paper across the short side of paper in different colors.
2. On each strip, have players write about:
   - A sad time
   - A happy time
   - Something or someone you miss
   - Something you're looking forward to
   - A time when someone or something died
   - A person you're glad was born
   - A time you were scared
   - A time you felt brave
   - A time you were lonely
   - A time you felt loved
3. Cut each strip into eight squares.
4. Rearrange them and glue them on another sheet of paper however you'd like.

LET'S TALK ABOUT IT!

Do you ever feel happy and sad at the same time when you think about someone or something you miss?

Resources

BOOKS

The Midlife Self Discovery Workbook by Lynn Louise Wonders is a great resource for parents or therapists to engage in self-care so they can be present for children.

Therapy Games for Teens by Kevin Gruzewski is a good tool if you enjoyed using these types of games but you also work with adolescents.

WEBSITES

Association for Play Therapy (a4pt.org) is a great site to learn more about play therapy or to search for a registered play therapist or play therapy supervisor in your area.

National Alliance on Mental Illness (NAMI.org) provides information on mental health issues as well as information on navigating the health care system if you think you need a therapist.

The National Suicide Prevention Lifeline (SuicidePreventionLifeline.org) can be reached through the chat feature on its website or by phone at 1-800-273-8255 for someone to talk to 24/7.

Stop Bullying (stopbullying.gov) offers information and suggestions for teaching children about bullying and provides tools for preventing it.

Index

C

D

E

F

G

T

U

ACKNOWLEDGMENTS

Thank you to Cam for listening to me talk about children's games incessantly for three months without complaining once and for joining in my excitement.

Thank you to my mentors (especially Lynn and Barbara), who were integral in my learning about play therapy and in gaining the confidence to start my own practice.

Thanks to Viva, who helped me cultivate the attitude and energy that I needed to have the mental space to write this book.

ABOUT THE AUTHOR

Christine Kalil, LICSW, RPT, is a licensed independent clinical social worker and registered play therapist in Washington, DC. She is the founder of DC Play Therapy, a private practice offering psychotherapy to children, adolescents, and adults. Kalil studied psychology at the University of Virginia and has been providing therapy to children and families since 2006. She has worked with clients in schools, hospitals, and homes and currently works in outpatient private practice. For more information about Christine Kalil or DC Play Therapy, visit DCPlayTherapy.com.